Prepare for 10 of life's unexpected stressful events

Kylie Parker

Foreword by
Eddie Lees

Copyright © 2018 by Kylie Parker

All rights reserved. This book or any portion thereof may not be reproduced or used in any manner whatsoever without the express written permission of the publisher except for the use of brief quotations in a book review.

Enquiries should be made to the publisher.

Printed in Australia

First Printing, 2018

ISBN 978-0-6482483-1-6

Published by:-
Planning Plan B Pty Limited
Suite 701C
Level 7
9-13 Bronte Road
Bondi Junction NSW 2022

www.planningplanb.com

DEDICATION

In the words of my children to whom I cannot imagine living without, **what does Planning Plan B mean?**

Lucas 10 – Plan B is when Plan A doesn't work, and you're left with one more plan . . . except for Plan C.

Jacob 13 - I don't know . . . it means planning something else? Can I write the back cover for you?

And from my "bonus" daughter Lindsay 7 – Can I draw a picture for the book?

They are why *I* need a Plan B. Why do *you* need a Plan B?

Foreword

Life is random.

That's my experience. During a long life, and having witnessed much that is inexplicable, the only conclusion that fits is this: much of what happens in life occurs randomly.

Mary wakes up one morning, relishing what looks like being a beautiful day. She addresses the quotidian issues: helping the family prepare for the next several hours or so; preparing herself for personal and business demands; for one meeting she runs early, for the next, she runs late; she's in control one minute and not quite in control the next; she makes calls and receives them; sends some messages and answers others; she stops for coffee, a smile and a chat before setting off again.

It's all busy, and mostly enjoyable – until it's not.

In the early evening, she learns of a disaster. It is deeply, deeply affecting. She can't take it all in. It begins to overwhelm. It drives many conflicting emotions simultaneously. Something needs to be done. She knows the why. But what? And when? And how? And who to call?

For any Mary, read any John. For the normal expectations of any day, read yours. For the disaster, read any challenge that life throws up, from the seriously inconvenient to the truly tragic.

That said, for many, life is an enjoyable journey: most of the lows are not too low and most of the highs are compensation for the beige bits in between. Yet we know that the unforeseeable is always out there – and, by definition, it strikes with unexpected suddenness.

This begs the question: if our normal expectations ('Plan A') fail for any reason, do we have a 'Plan B'? As a sizeable majority of us simply exist without the benefit of *any* set plan, it's highly unlikely that we have something remotely resembling a 'Plan B'.

Which brings us to what Kylie Parker has done with this remarkable book. She is a mother, a daughter, a homemaker, a professional accountant, a speaker - and now, an author. When Kylie went through a major personal setback, in addition to feeling bewildered and betrayed, she also felt very alone. She had never thought of having a Plan B – until life instructed her otherwise.

Part of her therapy was talking to others and in this she found that, while her experience was far from unique, the common denominator was that nobody she met had a Plan B either. That realisation became the genesis, the spark, and the motivation to write what you are about to read.

'Planning Plan B' is more than a book; it is a rich resource of help, with contributions from experts in different fields; it covers ten of the situations that can come at us from any direction, at any time. Kylie and her experts have assembled insights that will help every person who has the privilege to own a copy.

Life *is* random. And, with long hours and tireless energy, Kylie created *Planning Plan B* to help you cope.

Get reading. You'll be so glad you did.

Eddie Lees Founder, Now Sorted Pty Ltd
Proud to know Kylie Parker

Contents

Introduction ix
How does Planning Plan B help you in times of stress?

Chapter 1 1
The Holmes And Rahe Stress Scale

Chapter 2 8
Death

Chapter 3 24
Death of a spouse or close family member

Chapter 4 36
Divorce or permanent separation - without kids

Chapter 5 47
Divorce or permanent separation - with kids

Chapter 6 72
Disability or incapacity due to accident or illness

Chapter 7 84
Dismissal from employment

Chapter 8 97
Disaster occurring whilst travelling

Chapter 9 117
Dissolution of a business that is unforeseen
or due to financial losses

Chapter 10 134
Depression, mental illness or Dementia
References 154

Chapter 11 156
Distressed sale of home

Chapter 12 171
Documentation Checklist and Website links

Contributors to 'Planning Plan B' 181

In Memory Of 184

Acknowledgements 185

Introduction

"In preparing for battle I have always found that plans are useless, but planning is indispensable."

Dwight D. Eisenhower

Life unfortunately doesn't always go to Plan. Australians have a few sayings for when stressful events unexpectedly occur. They include: -

"It's gone tits up"
"It's gone pear shaped"
"The shit's hit the fan"

Though not eloquent, these describe the negative connotations around unexpected tragedies and the adverse impact they have on already busy and stressful lives.

Who needs Plan B when Plan A is awesome? I did.

The blood rushed to my feet as I grabbed the banister to keep from falling. I finally had evidence that my husband of 10 years and father to my two boys was having an affair with his younger work colleague. A careless moment in the rush to make a connecting flight resulted in him leaving his iPad in the kid's suitcase. This one message ended months of lies, counselling, a failed private investigator attempt, and confirmed that his raising the idea of divorcing did in fact relate to wanting to be with someone else.

To be fair to him, we had unofficially separated, but had agreed to be in the same home in different bedrooms until a month after our oldest son started a new school. I just thought with the absence of him wanting to be with someone else that he would see sense after a few months of living on his own and want to reconcile. Clearly that mangled fairy-tale ending didn't eventuate.

It had been several months earlier that, after a tough day at work, a scooter running into the back of my parked car on the way home (the rider unharmed), that I first received the mind-blowing news that my husband was no longer in love with me and wanted a divorce. I was blindsided. People say how can you not know, but if someone you love and trust, acts like they love you – you can't tell when they don't.

I confided in a close friend who was also my business partner, at an end of financial year work function. To try and help make me feel better, he shared in confidence that he had a mistress and had done so for the last nine months.

He and I had commenced business together in May 2005, when after 9 months of maternity leave I 'negotiated' a redundancy from the accounting firm I had worked at for eight years.

My new client base was growing, based on networking and referrals, and we soon made the decision to merge several separate accounting practices into one.

The new business commenced in July 2006. In the same month, I found I was pregnant with my second child; my then husband started a new job; my Grandfather died; a week after his funeral, my father was diagnosed with terminal cancer; and, in the middle of all this, we were undertaking a major home renovation. Sometimes our opportunities don't always align with perfect timing, but to say 'no' is something I still struggle with. My uncle has a saying: "*Bite off more than you can chew, and then chew like crazy*". At that time of my life, I was doing some seriously crazy chewing!

Given our prior professional relationships, and trust, we did have a business owner's agreement drawn up, but it never got past the draft stage.

With client growth, we grew from $2 million in fees, to an average of around $5.5 million and were in the BRW top 100 of Australian accounting firms - and part of a global accounting referral network.

Being responsible for our business development, marketing, HR and our own internal finances, I was heavily involved in the growth of our practice. Was it always easy with young children? Certainly not. But as an ownership team, we got on exceptionally well.

This unformalised business relationship worked brilliantly until I started to suspect my business partner was having his affair with one of our staff members. This created a real business concern.

The 'mistake' I made was just before Christmas 2014, when I advised a senior manager that it wasn't due to HR issues that I had become distant with the partner having the affair, it was because I didn't want to hear how many times he was seeing his mistress before work.

Well the 'proverbial' hit the fan when the senior manager went and told him straight away. I was called into an office with the other two older partners who, in clear terms told me I needed to fix this as the 'affair' partner was extremely annoyed. I was at fault for bringing a personal matter into our business.

The next day he and I talked, and whilst it was quite emotional I had hoped over time we could work through what had occurred.

We continued to remain civil to each other, however I was more concerned with ensuring my client commitments were being met and that my children were not emotionally hurt by what was happening with their own parents. With the Christmas holiday period coming up, my thoughts were that we would all have a break, and move on over time, given my personal life was still occupying my mind.

It was upon return from the holiday that I found the email message from my ex husbands work colleague to him . Based on the content of the message, and the 5 hours of reading their correspondence, while we had been away I asked my husband to move out on his return from his work conference. I threw myself into the internet: divorce articles, impact on children, coping with infidelity and RSVP, to keep from feeling the pain of betrayal and failure at not being able to raise my children in a loving marriage.

Six weeks after finding out my husband was in a relationship with someone else, my three male business partners called a board meeting on a Friday afternoon.

The conversation went along the lines of *'it pains me to have to do this but the business isn't going well and we have done the numbers and I think I will earn more if you leave.'*

I was responsible for the financial accounts the entire time we were in business and I knew this wasn't true, so I asked, *"Can I see your numbers"* only to receive in reply, *"they were done on the back of an envelope"*

The crux of the matter was that the partner having the affair had said to them 'either she goes, or I do' and they were concerned our previous friendship, which had irreparably broken down, would impact their business incomes.

I was fortunate that my internet online dating searches had resulted in the meeting of a nice guy a few weeks before. He had been through a similar work experience and I spent that first night in shock crying in his arms. His advice was sound, his empathy helping me to make the decision to keep moving forward.

Over the weekend, I thought about how I could start a new business with tax deadlines coming up, my manager going on maternity leave in a week, a divorce to emotionally and administratively work through, two young boys to help cope with the change, and no local family support. I made the decision to walk away from the business and put my health and kids first.

So, I called clients, advised them briefly of events, and was given office space with a friend where I was able to arrange the sale of my house, fully renovate a unit, prepare and lodge all the paperwork for our financial settlement, and then, with the support of clients, start a new business: Lotus Accountants – from the mud something beautiful grows

At the time of writing I still haven't been paid out by my previous business partners. To pursue this, I would be looking at a few hundred thousand in legal fees plus negative energy, when I was just trying to get my life back to normality for my kids – and it simply was not worth injuring my mental health any further. Had I had a formal business agreement, this process would have been much easier to pursue legally.

Given my personal life experiences and professional background I have written *Planning Plan B* so that, in the event someone else is ever blindsided by an unexpected stressful event, their stress is reduced through practical legal and financial planning.

How to prepare for unexpected stressful life events

It's impossible to predict if, when, and how an unexpected event will occur. However, anyone who watches the news knows that somewhere in the world things happen every day to negatively impact the course of life. The key question is: "Are you prepared if, one day, it is your family that is in the headlines?"

Unfortunately, there are few ways to prepare for some of the misfortune that we unexpectedly endure. For example, the death of a spouse - especially whilst raising young children - is almost always unanticipated. However, there are some things you can do to mitigate the stress and turmoil should the unexpected occur. They include:

- **Financial:** Lack of money is a major contributor to stress for many of the events in this book. To have a financial Plan B will help you feel more comfortable about money so that you may be able to avoid some of the negative implications associated with loss or change. Insurance policies and adequate coverage for debts and the raising of children provide enormous relief in the event a stressful event occurs.

- **Legal:** Working with your spouse to create an Estate Plan alleviates pressure on surviving family members. Where you have dependants or assets you should have Wills that state your wishes as to what you want to occur upon death. Should you be in business with someone, you have as much chance of this failing or having a falling out as you do a divorce. Divorce is one of the most common negative impacts on someone's wealth and health. Legal agreements need to be discussed and prepared for potential worst-case scenarios.
- **Social:** Studies have demonstrated that people with a better support network of friends and family also cope better emotionally with major stress in their lives. All too often the demands of raising a family result in the fracturing of friendships. Good relationships are what got me through some tough times and I ensure now, even in a new relationship, I make time to nurture them

Planning Plan B focuses on the financial and legal preparation that will mitigate some of the stress in the event of an unexpected life event occurring. Whilst the aim of this book isn't to depress or accentuate the negative, sticking your head in the sand won't help your family in the rare instance that dark things may happen; because, as you'll see, all too often they do.

If you love your family think of Plan A being for *you* and Plan B being for *them*. You can then be assured that you have done your best to look after those for whom you care most.

What to Plan for?

Thinking about disasters occurring is not a pleasant state of mind. I have a friend who used to always worry about her children dying, even commenting - supposedly as a joke - that she had a third as 'a spare'. The reality is that many things we *do* worry about aren't necessarily the ones that blindside us and throw our lives into turmoil.

In deciding what to write about, and plan for, I researched life's stressful events and came up with 10 all starting with 'D'. There are numerous negative words starting with D, so I have kept this as the theme for the 10 events chosen. I also reviewed the studies of two world renowned psychiatrists, Thomas Holmes and Richard Rahe, who developed the Holmes and Rahe Stress Scale in which each of the 10 events appear.

Chapter 1

The Holmes and Rahe Stress Scale

The Holmes Rahe Stress Scale was developed in the 1960s by psychiatrists Thomas Holmes and Richard Rahe. Together they studied the medical records of more than 5,000 people to analyse if stressful events in people's lives contributed to illness. The patients were asked to review a list of over 40 life events to determine if there was a correlation between these events and their illnesses.

The doctors continued their research and evaluation into the 1970s which continued to confirm that these events did have a negative impact on overall health. They devised a scoring method that allowed medical professionals to determine the probability of the development of illness in their patients based on their life-changing and stressful experiences.

The scale, called Life Changing Units, is very easy to measure. Simply indicate which of the events have occurred on the stress scale during a year and how often. The associated units are added up and the resulting score indicates the risk of developing illness. Scores of 300 or more result in a much higher risk of a serious illness while a score under 150 shows only slight risk.

Unfortunately, I personally experienced quite a few of those events in 2015; so, given the potential for increasing health issues, I am keen to ensure that my health is the number one priority in the next few years. Our health is all too often taken for granted and yet without it life and the ability to function independently and complete routine daily tasks can become impossible.

What adult life events are in the Top 10 of the Holmes and Rahe stress scale?

1. **Death of a spouse:** The death of a spouse is often far different from other end-of-life experiences. Financial implications are immediate and overwhelming. If children are involved, the experience can be even more traumatic as grief needs to take a backseat to survival. For this reason, the death of a spouse has a life changing unit of 100.

2. **Divorce:** Dropping down to a unit of 73, divorce has similar implications, but they are initiated by the actions of one or both parties. There are still financial implications, but long-term fighting can impact the divorcing spouses as well. There are also legal matters and additional costs. And when it comes to children, they can sadly find themselves in the middle of a major battle, where they are the ones who lose the most.

3. **Marital separation:** You don't even need to be officially divorced for a marital separation to impact both stress levels and overall health. While divorce is typically final, marital separation can end in reconciliation but the stress leading up to this decision can have a negative impact. The life changing units for a marital separation is 65.

4. **Imprisonment:** Incarceration for any reason for both yourself or family members can cause major issues for stress and illness. While many people believe that this is avoidable, there are reasons individuals can find themselves in trouble with the law for situations beyond their control or due to cultural factors that our society has yet to address. To dismiss the impact of these experiences on stress and health does a disservice to these individuals. It has life impact units of 63.

5. **Death of a close family member:** Also at 63 is the death of a close family member. There is no indication of how close or

who this individual would be in relation to the subject, so it can be assumed that anyone with whom the person had a close relationship could be counted in this experience. Grief can cause emotional stress that may impact multiple areas of someone's life.

6. **Personal injury or illness:** Half way down the list in the top ten most stressful life experiences on the Holmes Rahe Stress Scale is personal injury, or illness, with a value of 53. The impact of an injury or illness is often felt in loss of work, the feeling of being helpless, as well as issues with money relating to healthcare and insurance.

7. **Marriage:** While divorce and separation rank much higher on the scale, marriage itself can be very stressful. With life changing units of 50, marriage changes not only the relationship between two people but also the way society views their new relationship, the added pressures, learning to live with someone else and their habits and potential child raising responsibilities.

8. **Dismissal from work:** Job-related stress ranked at only 47 on the scale. Workplace stress is known to be a major cause of heart disease and hypertension. However, being fired from a job unexpectedly can be a larger contributor to stress and illness.

9. **Marital reconciliation:** Marriage holds several positions in the top ten life events, but it may be surprising to some people to see reconciliation at 45 units. Many people wrongly believe that getting back together with an estranged spouse will be the end of stress, but there are new implications on this already fragile relationship particularly where a spouse has been unfaithful.

10. **Retirement:** Lastly, at number ten on the scale is retirement at life changing units of 45. While some people dream of the time when they can retire and pursue aspects of their

lives they've always put on the back-burner, others are concerned about the financial impact of not working as well as the psychological feeling of no longer being needed or relevant.

Many of these events relate to our interaction with people close to us. In research conducted with refugees who have suffered through horrific acts, it is also events that occur to those they love most that causes the most distress.

After researching the Holmes and Rahe Stress Scale and trying to establish what it is possible to plan for, I made the decision to discuss events I knew about from a financial, pragmatic and personal experience perspective. These stresses come from either losing a loved or losing something that makes the lives of our loved ones more enjoyable.

Planning Plan B considers 10 stressful life events that can happen unexpectedly, which if planned for, would decrease the stress involved in the event they occur. The stressful ten are:

1. Death
2. Death of a spouse or close family member
3. Divorce or permanent separation– without kids
4. Divorce or permanent separation – with kids
5. Disability or incapacity due to accident or illness
6. Dismissal from employment
7. Disaster occurring whilst travelling
8. Dissolution of a business, due to financial loss or unforeseen events
9. Depression, mental illness or Dementia
10. Distressed sale of home

Holmes and Rahe Stress Scale

Task: Complete the Holmes and Rahe Stress Scale below

Holmes, T. H., & Rahe, R. H. (1967). The social readjustment rating scale. *Journal of psychosomatic research, 11, 213.*

HOLMES AND RAHE STRESS SCALE

Holmes and Rahe found that a score of 150 gives you a 50-50 chance of developing an illness. A score of 300+ gives you a 90% chance of developing an illness, having an accident or "blowing up". Notice that "positive times" like Christmas, marriage and vacations are stressful.

multiply event by the number of times you have experienced it in the last year

#	LIFE EVENT (STRESSOR)	VALUE	#/YR	TOTAL
1	DEATH OF SPOUSE	100 X		=
2	DIVORCE	73 X		=
3	MARITAL SEPARATION	65 X		=
4	JAIL TERM	63 X		=
5	DEATH OF CLOSE FAMILY MEMBER	63 X		=
6	MAJOR PERSONAL INJURY OR ILLNESS	53 X		=
7	MARRIAGE	50 X		=
8	FIRED FROM WORK	47 X		=
9	MARITAL RECONCILIATION	45 X		=
10	RETIREMENT	45 X		=
11	MAJOR CHANGE IN HEALTH OF FAMILY MEMBER	44 X		=
12	PREGNANCY	40 X		=
13	SEX DIFFICULTIES	39 X		=
14	GAIN OF NEW FAMILY MEMBER	39 X		=
15	MAJOR BUSINESS READJUSTMENT	39 X		=
16	MAJOR CHANGE IN FINANCIAL STATE	38 X		=
17	DEATH OF CLOSE FRIEND	37 X		=
18	CHANGE TO DIFFERENT LINE OF WORK	36 X		=
19	MAJOR CHANGE IN NUMBER OF ARGUMENTS WITH SPOUSE	35 X		=
20	MORTGAGE OVER $100,000	31 X		=
21	FORCLOSURE OF MORTAGE OR LOAN	30 X		=
22	MAJOR CHANGE IN RESPONSIBILITIES AT WORK	29 X		=
23	SON OR DAUGHTER LEAVING HOME	29 X		=
24	TROUBLE WITH IN-LAWS	29 X		=
25	OUTSTANDING PERSONAL ACHIEVEMENT	28 X		=
26	SPOUSE BEGINS OR STOPS WORK	26 X		=
27	BEGIN OR END SCHOOL	26 X		=
28	MAJOR CHANGE IN LIVING CONDITIONS	25 X		=
29	REVISION OF PERSONAL HABITS	24 X		=
30	TROUBLE WITH BOSS	23 X		=
31	MAJOR CHANGE IN WORK HOURS OR CONDITIONS	20 X		=
32	CHANGE IN RESIDENCE OR SCHOOLS	20 X		=
33	MAJOR CHANGE IN RECREATION	19 X		=
34	MAJOR CHANGE IN CHURCH ACTIVITIES	19 X		=
35	MAJOR CHANGE IN SOCIAL ACTIVITIES	18 X		=
36	MORTGAGE OR LOAN LESS THAN $10,000	17 X		=
37	MAJOR CHANGE IN SLEEPING HABITS	16 X		=
38	MAJOR CHANGE IN NUMBER OF FAMILY GET-TOGETHERS	15 X		=
39	MAJOR CHANGE IN EATING HABITS	15 X		=
40	VACATIONS, CHRISTMAS	13 X		=
41	MINOR VIOLATIONS OF THE LAW	11 X		=
			YOUR TOTAL	

OPINIONS AND FEELINGS ARE FREQUENTLY A PERSONAL TRIUMPH OVER GOOD THINKING
YOU DEFINE REALITY BY WHAT YOU KNOW, WHAT YOU BELIEVE, AND WHAT YOU DO ABOUT IT.

How did you score?

The Holmes and Rahe Stress scale features 41 incidents that will cause stress, on a scale from 11 - 100. Each item is assigned a value, multiplied by the number of times it has occurred in a year; when you add up the value of the events that have affected you, there is a score that can indicate your risk factor for developing illnesses.

Results

Less than 150 life change units you have a 30% chance of suffering from stress.

150 - 299 life change units equate to a 50% chance of suffering from stress.

Over 300 life units means you have an 80% chance of developing a stress related illness.

Should you obtain a Total of over 300 it would be advisable to speak with a medical professional to determine if you need to be taking any specific actions.

Your score	
Your spouse	
Other score	

Plan B Fund

To help in the event you are impacted by one of these events consider creating a Plan B savings fund. Time is the greatest gift for accumulating wealth to assist with financial turmoil, should it occur, and it only takes small amounts started at a young age to grow to a considerable amount in later years.

Imagine if you smoke a packet of cigarettes per day how quitting and saving that would add up over 10 years. At a current average of

$25 per pack that equates to $91,250 - and that doesn't even factor in what would be added with interest and investment returns.

What about chocolate, wine, beer, shoes – all the items spent discretionally, that we can live without? What could you save with the benefit of accumulation and time that might be utilised in the event of an unexpected negative event occurring?

If you have a joint authority account, you are less likely to dip into funds; left to grow, you could then look at other investment opportunities, such as managed funds, shares or higher yield deposits, to build the amount.

Key take-away:

Stress has an impact on just about every aspect of life. Try to understand what causes it and do your best to avoid it – read this chapter again later if need be and do your own online research on how to avoid and, at least, cope with the stress factors in your own life.

CHAPTER 2

DEATH

"Death is nothing to us, since when we are, death has not come, and when death has come, we are not."

Epicurus

Death

It is said there are only three certainties in life: birth, taxes and death. And yet most of us do our best to ignore our inevitable demise, thereby failing to plan adequately for the family and friends we leave behind.

Even when people are told they have a terminal illness, with only months to live, the will to live is so strong that miracle cures and options are considered above and beyond the acceptance and preparation for one's death.

While our ultimate passing is something we don't wish to dwell upon, should the worst-case scenario occur it's worth thinking for a moment about how family and loved ones would cope. Imagine their emotional suffering at that time. They will likely will be irrational, inconsolable and unable to think straight, finding even ordinary day to day routines insurmountable.

Notwithstanding being emotionally stretched, tired, deeply upset and in shock, it's at this very point in their lives that the following key items need to be organised:

1. Obtain a Doctor's Certificate of Cause of Death
2. Determine whether you registered with a government organisation your decision on organ donation
3. Notify your friends, family, work colleagues, clients and decide which communication channels
4. Find and review insurance policies to determine if you had a policy that covered funeral and other expenses
5. Find your Will to determine if you had any clauses relating to your funeral arrangements, a pre-paid funeral plan, or specific wishes around cremation, burial, service and type of coffin
6. Engage a funeral director
7. Access your bank accounts, particularly whether in joint names because these may become problematic for spouses to access
8. Review social media accounts and close or change their usage as either indicated in the will or as emotionally best for your family
9. Prepare for the funeral service – it has often been said a wedding with the same number of people takes months to prepare and yet a funeral needs preparation within days
10. Advise relevant government authorities of your death

11. Arrange the preparation of your final tax return
12. Review any business structures and change details in conjunction with professional advisors
13. Sort through your personal effects and make decisions on their subsequent allocation or disposal

As the list goes on – the items above comprise just some of the steps necessary after you have passed on - you may imagine the burden placed on family, and particularly your spouse, as being among the most stressful events in their life. Emotional turmoil, financial pressure and the normal hassles of everyday life help to explain how people slide into depression following the death of their spouse.

Considering this list, you would surely want to reduce this burden in any way you could. Whilst this book is designed to help you in *Planning Plan B* (and, let's face it, there is no option against ultimately dying) you *can* help those around you by mitigating the trauma of your passing.

The depth and detail of your preparation will depend on your individual situation; generally, the more complicated your personal financial and family situation, the more I would recommend you seek the services of an expert in estate planning.

So, unless you believe in cryogenics, I recommend you start planning for what needs to happen *after* your death to assist loved ones at the time of their grieving.

How do you plan for your Estate?

The word Estate recalls an English lord living in a manor with a large land holding, where peasants obediently toiled away for him. Estate ownership was kept in the family by being passed down to the eldest son (known as primogeniture). This is where the word Estate originated.

Estate is the term officially used to describe everything comprising the net worth of an individual, including all land, possessions and other assets. Should you have a legal obligation to look after and provide for minor children, invalid parents or other dependants, you also need to plan for their care in the unfortunate event that something happens to you.

An Estate Plan primarily includes a Will as well as any other directions on how you want your assets distributed after your death. It should also include papers that legally document how you will be cared for, medically and financially, if you become unable to make your own decisions in the future.

You must be over 18 and mentally competent when you have the required legal agreements prepared that form your Estate Plan.

Standard documents in Australia often include:

- Will
- Superannuation death nomination
- Testamentary trust
- Powers of attorney
- Power of guardianship
- Statement of Wishes

Warning: If you have made a binding death nomination in your superannuation or insurance policies, the beneficiaries named in those policies will override anyone mentioned in your will.

Warning: If you have a family trust, the trust continues, and its assets will be distributed according to the trust deed. It is important, though, to ensure the position of the Trustee is planned for if it currently identifies you as a Director of a company or you are an individual Trustee.

A well-drawn up Estate Plan will ensure that:

- Tax payable is minimised on the income earned from the assets and any capital gains from their sale.
- The right amount of ownership and control of your assets passes to your intended beneficiaries; and
- Your assets are protected if a nominated beneficiary is involved in legal difficulties such as divorce, bankruptcy or other unanticipated issues.

Prepare a Will

A Will comes into effect when you die and, notwithstanding scenes in movies, it is rare in Australia to have the formal Will read in front of family members. It includes items such as how your assets will be shared, who will look after your children if they are still young, what trusts you want established, if any, how much money you'd like donated to charities and even instructions about your funeral.

Your Will can be written and updated by private trustees and/or solicitors, who usually charge a fee. The nature and complexity of your estate invariably determines who is professionally best suited to assist with your Will.

Family trusts, pay-out of superannuation balances and the tax implications for beneficiaries can all be managed within a carefully considered estate planning exercise.

It's estimated that nearly half of all Australians die 'intestate', that is, without a Will. When this happens, the government will decide how your estate is administered.

The government will only take your assets if there are no living next of kin, however it is still worth considering charitable bodies before leaving your assets to the government.

Each state in Australia has its own intestacy laws which reflect what happens to your estate if you do not have a valid Will.

You can also buy Will kits online but it's a good idea to ask a solicitor to review your Will to make sure everything is in order. If a Will isn't signed and witnessed properly, it will be invalid and therefore despite your best intentions, your wishes may not be carried out.

Ensure your Will is relevant, valid and up to date as your legal rights change, specifically if you marry, divorce or separate; have children or grandchildren; if your spouse or beneficiaries die; or if you have a significant change in financial circumstances.

Warning: Consider any potential areas for conflict amongst the distribution of your estate to the nominated beneficiaries. If you have a blended family, ex-spouse, dependants, estranged children and don't feel comfortable talking to them about what you have planned then chances are they will challenge your Will. Clear directions and communication around any of these issues are advised to be carried out to avoid your loved ones being drawn into a court process.

Explaining any unpopular decisions in regards to your asset distribution will reduce the risk of your Will being contested.

The Executor

An extremely important role in your Will is that of your Executor. He, or she, or them, will oversee carrying out your wishes as you have legally documented them. Often people choose their closest friend or their children although this might not be in the best interest of all concerned.

Executors are responsible for organising the funeral, applying for probate, finding and identifying the assets, identifying and paying all the liabilities and expenses including tax, distributing the net assets and dealing with any disputes between beneficiaries or challenges to the Will. For the non-professional, it can be a very demanding and responsible role.

Given the serious nature of the role consider the following questions before you choose an Executor for your Will: -

1. Do they have experience in dealing with administration and financial matters?
2. Will they be available to make the time to perform the duties required?
3. Are they willing to undertake the role?
4. If you make the Executors your children– do they all get along?
5. Are they in a stable situation – bankruptcy, divorce, drugs and alcohol problems could have a major impact on their ability to carry out this role. It is possible that even if your children are not directly involved, their partners might have significant influence, and this can put undue pressure on the executor's role.

While there is no legal requirement for the future executor to be formally advised of the role, it is a highly recommended to obtain their approval and permission first.

Should they refuse, or be unable to act, or pre-decease you, the beneficiaries are likely to suffer much inconvenience, cost, stress and delays. Whilst the "Will" remains valid, as there is no one to automatically step in to do the administration, it will have to wait until the Supreme Court appoints someone (usually one of the beneficiaries) into the role. So, it is important that you inform and educate the executor as to what the likely duties will be and obtain their agreement to act in this capacity.

It is also important to be aware of State based requirements for the Executor to live in the same State as the deceased, if this is not the case your beneficiaries may need to appoint someone else or the Public Trustee slowing down the legal administration.

Binding Death benefit nomination

Superannuation is not considered an estate asset. On death, it doesn't automatically flow to the estate of the deceased. The trustee of the super fund will generally pay a death benefit in accordance with the governing rules of the fund and the relevant law. A binding death benefit nomination is the only way to override this trustee discretion.

Given this is an area that is quite complex, it is outside the scope of this book to provide advice and we suggest you seek the services of a qualified professional to ensure your assets pass to intended beneficiaries in the most tax effective means possible.

Testamentary trusts

A testamentary trust is a trust set out in a Will and only takes effect when the person who has created the Will dies. Testamentary trusts are usually set up to protect assets however be mindful of your reasons for doing so to avoid "controlling from the grave".

Here are some reasons why you would create a testamentary trust:

- The beneficiaries are minors (under 18 years old)
- The beneficiaries have diminished mental capacity
- You do not trust the beneficiary to use their inheritance wisely
- You do not want family assets split as part of a divorce settlement
- You do not want family assets to become part of bankruptcy proceedings

A trust will be administered by a trustee who is usually appointed in the Will.

A trustee must look after the assets for the benefit of the beneficiaries until the trust expires and in accordance with the clauses in the Trust Deed.

The expiry date of a trust will be a specific date such as when a minor reaches a certain age, or a beneficiary achieves a certain goal or milestone, like getting married or attaining a specific qualification as outlined in the Trust Deed.

Powers of attorney

Appointing someone as your power of attorney gives them the legal authority to look after affairs on your behalf.

The types of Powers of attorney (PoA) depend on which state or territory you are in: they can refer to just financial powers, or they might include broader guardianship powers. They all become invalid upon the death of the person as the Executor then is in control of the Estates Assets.

There are different types of PoAs:

1. A **general power of attorney** is where you appoint someone to make financial and legal decisions for you, usually for a specified period; for example, if you're overseas and need someone to complete the purchase of a house. This person's appointment becomes invalid if you lose the capacity to make decisions for yourself.
2. An **enduring power of attorney** is where you appoint a person to make financial and legal decisions for you even if you lose the capacity to make your own decisions.
3. A **medical power of attorney** can make only medical decisions on your behalf if you become unable to do so yourself.

You can prepare a few other documents to help your legal appointees and family as you grow older, including:

- An **enduring power of guardianship** that gives a person the right to choose where you live and make decisions about

your medical care and other lifestyle choices, if you lose the capacity to make your own decisions.
- An **anticipatory direction** records your wishes about medical treatment in the future, in case you become unable to express those wishes yourself.
- An **advance healthcare directive (or 'living will')** documents how you would like your body to be dealt with if you lose the capacity to make those decisions yourself and includes the first two objectives. These forms and instructions can be found online through various State Government departments.

Digital Life

When I first became an accountant one of my first jobs was helping with the estate of a client. I went to his home, his wife showed me where the filing cabinet was, and I went to work sorting through the paper documents to compile a statement of his assets and liabilities.

That same task, now given online shares, passwords, trading sites and multiple accounts can be near impossible if you don't have a Plan B for your online life. This difficult issue has created a new area around creating a Digital Will.

Create a Digital Will

Have you ever wondered what will happen to your social media accounts when you die? How do you want your family and friends to remember you? What information might you have that you don't want to impact negatively on your loved ones when you are no longer around to protect them from access?

If you have a computer, mobile phone or tablet you have a digital life. This virtual life is intrinsically linked to your real world and so needs the same level of planning for unexpected death or incapacity.

Internet Banking and Financial Assets

Each banking institution has its own 'deceased' policy and can generally be found simply by searching for "internet banking and death". Do you know what happens to your joint bank accounts if something happens to your spouse? Do your children even know what accounts you have and with which bank? What about superannuation accounts, Bitcoin, shares? Just think about the accounts you log into daily – who else knows how to access this information?

James Howells made the news in 2013 after he discovered that he had inadvertently thrown out hard drives containing 7,500 Bitcoins. When this was reported, the amount was estimated at $7.5 million; at the time of writing this is worth $13.8 million. Imagine a departed relative was in possession of millions of dollars of digital assets that you were unable to access and that these assets remain unclaimed, indefinitely.

Social Media

Unfortunately, there is not a 'one size fits all' solution to social media. Each social media platform, whether it be Facebook, Twitter, Instagram, Google or the like, has its own rules on deletion, deactivation, data downloading and memorialisation. If you are concerned about your privacy, then consider how you want to treat each of these if you are no longer able to operate the accounts.

Photos

The last time I had photos printed for an album was in 2010. Every New Year's Eve I resolve to print them out but the day to day busyness takes over and another year of thousands of photos remain on my phone, laptop or, if lucky, saved to an online document storage program.

Where are all your photos and memories stored? In online printing places, Facebook, online document storage, iCloud? There are so many places now who will keep your special memories once you are gone and how will they access them.

Intellectual Property (IP)

Considering I have a domain name buying obsession how many other people have IP that is now only digitally accessed? I have over 33 domain names and one day those may very well be valuable; however, if no one else knows I have them they will sit in cyberspace unless not renewed, and then go back into circulation.

Documentation – Estate Plan

The documents you choose to draw up will depend on your personal circumstances, and the defined responsibilities you are happy to entrust to others.

Please seek legal advice, particularly as mentioned, if you have assets, minors, dependants, or have investments or interests overseas that may require an International Will to be prepared.

Once your paperwork is in order, it will help your executor and family if you list the legal documents you have and where they are kept.

Keeping a record of your personal information and notes on how your legal documents, assets and investments are arranged can also help you. Saving documents either in a secure online folder, safe or purpose-built application like Now Sorted (www.nowsorted.com) is strongly recommended.

Key documents to keep:
- Birth certificate
- Marriage certificate
- Will
- Passport
- Enduring power of attorney
- Advance healthcare directive (also called a living will)
- Personal insurance policies
- House deeds or mortgage documents
- Home and contents insurance

- Deeds and insurance policies for any other real estate you own
- Bank account details
- Superannuation papers
- Investment documents (securities, share certificates, bonds)
- Medicare card
- Medical insurance details
- Pensioner concession card
- Any pre-payments of funeral investments
- Details of computer records
- Contact details of your accountants, lawyer and financial planner
- Passwords
- Motor Vehicle registration papers

By intelligent planning, think not only of the end of *your* life but of the family and loved ones you leave behind. Don't you think they deserve to have life made easier at their time of loss and mourning?

Do you have the following documentation?	Yes or No	Action to take	By when?
Will			
Binding death benefit nomination (superannuation)			
Power of Attorney			
Enduring Power of Attorney (money)			
Appointment of enduring guardian (family and health)			
Advanced Care/Health Directive			
Life insurance policy			
Online passwords stored securely			
Contact details for who or where the above information is stored			

Key take-away:

Although developed societies have done their best to sanitise death in recent decades, the fact is that none of us is immune – and, as can be seen, it can be a very complex subject. At least now, however, you have some guide notes on how to deal with this matter which, to the consternation of many, has too often become a taboo topic. That said, the more you know, the better you will be able to cope. The story on Prince, the musician, is instructive.

The Story of Prince and the missing Will

On 21 April 2016, along with millions of others who grew up listening to Prince, I was shocked to learn that he had died at age 57. He was found alone and unresponsive in an elevator at Paisley Park. For someone who controlled his assets so closely during his life time, as evidenced by the trademarks he held, including for the insignia he used, it was amazing to learn that he did not have a Will.

Whilst he clearly wasn't planning to die suddenly, the fact that someone with such wealth, estimated at over $300 million, didn't plan for its distribution was clearly a "Let's go crazy" moment.

Prince is not the only celebrity to die Intestate. Jimi Hendrix, Kurt Cobain, Amy Winehouse - all had unexpected deaths that left family members having to deal with the court system on top of their grief.

After his death, Michael Hutchence's family members were embroiled in court battles, apparently due to the lack of information on his financial position when he passed away.

All these are public examples of the issues that arise when someone dies without planning for what happens to their estate or dependants. I can't imagine Michael ever thought his daughter would be raised by Sir Bob Geldof; nor Sir Bob Geldof raising his ex-wife's child. Not exactly a Plan A scenario.

1. The following is a true and correct inventory at date of death values of all the property of the Estate, both real and personal, which has come into my possession as Personal Representative. If an appraisal of any asset has been made, the name and address of each appraiser used is included. After diligent search and inquiry concerning the assets of the Estate, the following is a list of the Estate assets by category:

SCHEDULE			VALUE
Schedule A:	Real Estate		$ 25,431,900.00
Schedule B:	Stocks, Bonds, and Other Securities		$ 0.00
Schedule C:	Bank Accounts, Mortgages, Contracts for Deed, Notes and Cash		$ 110,080.51
Schedule D:	Other Personal Property		$ 836,166.70
	SUBTOTAL		$ TBD
Less Schedule E:	Mortgages and Liens		$ 0.00
	TOTAL		$ TBD

Prince was married and divorced twice. His first marriage produced two children, with the eldest boy being born with a skeletal abnormality known as Pfeiffer's Syndrome and dying seven days after he was born. There was also a miscarriage.

As Prince died without a spouse, children or instructions for his asset distribution, the allocation to his heirs became subject to determination by a court as to the beneficiaries and a matter for public record.

http://www.mncourts.gov/mncourtsgov/media/CIOMedia Library/Documents/Inventory.pdf

The link above and the summary lists an inventory schedule of his personal belongings at the time of his death. Whilst it is interesting to be able to review this document, one must wonder if an entertainer's privacy isn't something that should be valued as highly in death as it should be in life?

Below are the vehicles he owned; quite conservative really and not what I expected.

1993 Ford Thunderbird (MN)	1995 Jeep Grand Cherokee (MN)
1997 Lincoln Town Car (MN)	2004 Cadillac Roadster XLR (MN)
2010 Mercedes Benz	2011 Lincoln MKT (MN)
1996 BMW Z3 Roadster (MN)	2006 Bentley (CA)
1985 Cadillac Limo (MN)	1999 Plymouth Prowler (MN)

While Prince left millions of fans grieving, because of a lack of planning he now has one sibling and five half siblings making collective decisions on how future recordings will be released. With over 30 people being dismissed by the Judge in their claims to being heirs the case is one of the most complicated estate cases in Minnesota.

Among other would-be heirs the Judge denied five people who came forward claiming Prince was their biological or adoptive father, and several others claiming their Dad was also Prince's genetic parent by way of an extramarital affair with his mother.

Quotes in the press have legal fees already around $2.8 million and with the assets still yet to be released this is an ongoing legal battle that could have been so easily avoided.

Chapter 3

Death of a spouse or close family member

"The life of the dead is placed in the memory of the living."

Marcus Tullius Cicero

Death of a spouse or close family member

The degree of emotional stress and recovery from the loss of a spouse or a close family member is individually experienced.

The impact varies based on age, relationship, financial dependency, and how the information on either a terminal illness or an unexpected accident is delivered.

This book does not cover the emotional side of coping with the dying process of someone you love – that's better left to experts in psychology and psychiatry.

However, having experienced the loss of my own father through cancer, as well as losing my brother in law at the age of 31 (who had two young children), I have found that the demands of everyday life inevitably inhibit the healing process.

When grief is not properly dealt with, it tends to have an impact on other aspects of life, so please seek professional assistance to help with the grieving process.

The aim of this chapter is to help plan for the practical and financial implications of the death of a close family member and the presumption is you have read the detail in Chapter Two.

Spouse

The death of a spouse brings emotional and financial turmoil. Joint bank accounts can be frozen, pension payments reduced and, often, the loss of a sole provider's income.

Frequently in relationships, one person administers the finances and the other is content to just withdraw from the ATM. If you are the ATM withdrawer, then this is for you!

Preparing for your death (in the preceding chapter) will help those closest to you but how do you approach preparation for a spouse's death if (either through superstition, unpleasant thoughts, or thinking they might 'jinx' themselves) they don't want to plan for it?

Hopefully, the contents of this book create a context for starting a conversation that leads to a Plan B being prepared.

Ideas to start a conversation

- *Leave the book on your bedside table*
  Curiosity will generally result in the question being asked as to why you are reading this book. Explain that you are unsure of your current financial situation and, should something unexpectedly happen, you want to be prepared.

- *Directly ask*

    Do we have: Wills? Life insurance? A plan to cover our children's education and living expenses? A list of our professional advisers (accountant, lawyer, etc.)?

    Tip: go back and read the list in Chapter Two - the knowledge you obtain will help start the discussion with your spouse.

- *Tell a story*

    Explain how you heard about someone losing their spouse and they didn't have any insurance and so then they also had to sell their home. Relate the negative impact this had on the person and how you don't want that to happen to your family.

- *Seek the advice of an expert*

    Make an appointment to see an estate planning lawyer and have them help with engaging your spouse in estate planning preparation.

    Tip: Once you have agreed to have a family discussion around estate planning then the items in Chapter Two need to be addressed for all parties ... and securely stored.

Child

The loss of a child is one of the most horrific life events and I am surprised it's not on the top of the Holmes and Rahe stress scale.

As my ex father in law came out from viewing his 31-year-old son at the funeral home he just burst into tears and said, "you just never think you will outlive your children"

Unfortunately, I have been to too many funerals where I have watched parents grieve over the loss of their child, tragically and unexpectedly lost.

No one ever tells you before having children that they can make you feel so emotionally vulnerable. Crying because something has happened to a child around the same age as your own is not uncommon.

Given this vulnerability, it maybe the first time an individual actually does care about what happens when they die. The birth of a child may prompt you to see an insurance advisor, prepare a Will or discuss organ donation. Whilst a large percentage of people who pre-plan their estate do so for their children, the impact financially of a child dying is often overlooked.

Questions to consider in losing a child may include the following: -

- How will you get up each day and go to work as if everything is the same?
- Will your income be affected?
- What is the impact on siblings? Will they need counselling?
- How will your relationship handle the stress and grief given there is an increased risk of divorce after the loss of a child?
- Are you able to have more children or is this perhaps now not possible?
- Do you have Life insurance for your children? This is generally available in amounts up to $100,000 however is not designed to replace a lost income in the event you are not able to work for several months.

I have heard parents comment that life is never the same following the loss of a child; never a day goes by you don't think of them, but you just keep on having to keep on anyway.

Concerns around a child's safety

A high conflict divorce or separation can add anxiety concerning your child whilst in the other parent's care. This is outside the scope of Planning Plan B. Should you have concerns about your child's safety there are numerous support groups and links in NAPCAN (National Association for Prevention of Child Abuse and Neglect) that will provide you with information to help. http://napcan.org.au/urgent-help/

Parent

The impact of a loss of a parent varies depending on your relationship, age and financial dependency.

With life expectancies having now reached the 80's, and beyond, and people having children later in life (especially second marriages) there exists a period where you may need to look after young children *and* elderly parents. This state of 'being in the middle' is often described as belonging to the "sandwich" generation.

Again, questions need to be asked around who will care for aging parents and young children?

Medical visits and expenses involve time and money. How will this be practically facilitated in the event care is required?

I have a friend who now lives in Switzerland who has been spending substantial amounts of time in Australia caring for her terminally ill parent. I, too, spent 18 months with two young toddlers, a renovation and a new business, simultaneously helping with the support of my father when he was diagnosed with terminal cancer – all while I was living 2 ½ hours away from him.

The strain and burden on relationships, health and mental wellbeing when caring for someone whom you know is dying is anything but easy. And the uncertainty around when they will die creates another kind of anxiety around planning your own life. Holidays become harder to consider 'in case something happens 'while you are a long distance away; personal obligations, work conferences, celebrations - these all need to be given more thought than under 'normal' circumstances.

Conversations with aging parents also become more difficult. This is largely because of the awkwardness of being perceived as selfishly thinking of the inheritance. How do you broach a subject with a parent without seeming to be highly indelicate? Not an easy conversation to start, which is even more reason you should have a clear Estate Plan and ensure it is communicated so those that you love most are not left conflicting with siblings or other close family members following anyone's death, including your own.

Sibling

I watched first-hand the grieving of my first husband when he learnt of his brother's accidental death in a motor bike accident in April, 1994. We had only been married three months and as I watched the family close ranks, there almost seemed a hierarchy of who had the greater right to grieve. It was certainly not deliberate but being young, none of us even thought at the time about the future impact this accidental death would have on all the people he knew.

Those greatly impacted were: his wife, his two children (who were 7 and 5), his mother, his father, his brother and sister, aunties and uncles, cousins, friends and then in laws. Often your own grief is set to the side because of a feeling to be strong for someone who has a perceived right to grieve more. In my instance it was to be strong and help with the children, so at 21 I was fielding questions, while the family members told stories in another room, about his life, about God and heaven - from two sweet, bewildered children, only nights after their father's death.

In fact, when I searched for resources regarding grief for a sibling, there was a distinct lack of information available.

This is just a feeling based on my personal experiences, but sibling grief is often overshadowed. People simply cannot fathom the unique distress of a parent having to bury a child. The thoughts of a sibling are often of the parent's grief. Parents themselves may not be able to effectively attend to their children's grief - and peripheral family and friends may be hesitant to step in and offer support or suggestions.

My experience was that support and attention was first given to siblings who were younger or who were perceived to be more fragile. In a situation where this occurs a grieving sibling may end up feeling as though other people's grief is more important than their own and supress their own grief.

This may be compounded by the fact that some people willingly allow their grief to go unnoticed by themselves or others. It is important for all members of the family to recognise that no one's grief should take complete precedence. Although family members might take turns supporting one another, at one point or another everyone's grief deserves attention and needs to be recognised for its depth.

My father also once made a comment to me: never judge someone's grieving process or expect that it might be rational. This is the best advice I ever had in relation to helping someone grieve. Don't judge, just be there.

Do your close family members have the following documentation?	Yes or No	Action to take	By when?
Will			
Binding death benefit nomination (superannuation)			
Power of Attorney			
Enduring Power of Attorney (money)			
Appointment of enduring guardian (family and health)			
Advanced Care/Health Directive			
Life insurance policy			
Online passwords stored securely			
Contact details for who or where the above information is stored			

Key take-away:

These notes are aimed at a more specific understanding of what happens following the death of someone close to you ... we think you will find this chapter an invaluable resource if or when such an event occurs within your experience.

10 Questions for an Expert

Financial Planners Mark Bradley & Hamish Thomson from Priority Advisory Group

1) **I want to insure my spouse in case something happens to them how do I do this and what amount should I insure their life for?**

   The first thing to do would be to have this discussion with your spouse. Pick your time well, just after they have started a particularly hazardous pursuit is probably a good segue…If they have already been admitted to intensive care this is probably a bit late. As to how much, well that depends. General consensus is that you would want to clear any debts the family may have and then have sufficient capital remaining to generate an income for your family for as long as is necessary, taking children's ages into account, your ability to work etc. You would want to speak to a financial adviser who would have the necessary tools to calculate the amount based on your family's needs and objectives. Check your spouse's existing cover in their Super, you may not need to have that discussion after all.

2) **Am I able to organise life insurance myself online to cover my spouse?**

   Absolutely, you can go online. You can get anything online these days. Being a vital part of your family's financial security, I'd suggest getting an expert to ensure that the solution that you get will work as you have planned and, ideally, having that person available to assist your family in the event of a claim. It's rather difficult for you to answer any questions the online provider may have for you, in the event they need to clarify what you put in your online application, once you have passed on. Also, research has shown that direct insurance can be more expensive than advised insurance. http://riskinfo.com.au/news/2017/05/22/direct-insurance-pegged-back-by-lapses/

3) **What do I need to consider for our minor children as I work full time and would need help to be able to look after them?**

   These are additional costs that need to be accounted for when determining the income required (See number 1) Childcare and education expenses, (current and future), an au pair, additional travel expenses and the fact that you may not be able to work the same number of hours, all contribute to extra life cover being required to fund these expenses.

4) **What happens if my spouse doesn't have a will and all our bank accounts and home are in joint names?**

   A "right of survivorship" applies to joint assets. Where assets are jointly owned and one co-owner dies, the share of the deceased person passes automatically to the surviving co-owner. The effect is as though the deceased person never held the share in the asset. Obviously, this would be different if the assets were owned as tenants in common. A prudent course of action would be get some advice and if necessary ascertain exactly how your assets are owned and, if necessary, have the ownership arrangement changed.

5) **I have a fractured family and am worried that if one of our parents die we will fight as one of my siblings lives with them still and has no money. Is there a way we can reduce the risk of our family fighting when our parents pass away?**

   It's always better to resolve and get agreement on these issues when everyone is still alive and preferably talking to each other. Seek advice from a specialist estate planning Solicitor, outline the family dynamic and request that they draft robust Estate Planning documentation. Also discuss with a Financial Adviser the potential need for an 'Estate equalisation' payment and how this may be funded. If it is possible to get life insurance this can be used to equalise the estate, eg the sibling staying at home could inherit the property and the other siblings could get cash from the proceeds of the policy.

6) **If the person I love has decided to donate their organs, but I didn't know about this can I have that request overruled?**

Yes, in Australia the family will always be asked to confirm the donation decisions of the deceased before donation for transplantation can proceed. Although family objection is always tested to ensure that it is an informed decision, donation does not proceed if a family strongly objects.

http://www.donatelife.gov.au/ota-position-statement-legal-framework-consent-donation

7) **We have a few superannuation policies from different employers over the years and want to merge them, what should we consider?**

Consider whether consolidation will result in the loss of benefits or entitlements you may wish to retain. Consider if there will be overall reduction in costs. Even if the costs are the same it may be worth the effort just for the increased simplicity of dealing with one provider. Different providers may give you the benefit of different investment strategies, thereby adding an additional layer of diversification to your Super investments.

8) **How long will it take until I can sort out all the paperwork if my family member dies?**

Most estates are finalised within 9-12 months. The minimum time to finalise an estate is 6 months from the date of death. If the executor distributes the estate before this time they are not protected if claims are made against the estate.

9) **What professional advice should I seek when someone dies and how do I find an expert?**

The better strategy would be to have an expert advising you before any disastrous events. You will require legal and financial advice. Begin by seeking out the professional advisers the deceased had engaged most recently (Financial Advisors and/or Accountants).

If they had not engaged such professionals, ask friends and family if they know Solicitors or Financial Advisers/ Accountants whose services they would endorse.

10) **Is there anything else I should consider in the event I die that will help reduce the stress of my loved ones based on your experience?**

Ensuring your loved ones have a good knowledge of your wishes will reduce some of their emotional stress. On a practical level, ensuring your record keeping is complete and up to date will help avoid additional stress. It is a good idea to have as complete records as possible including the obvious things like all your bank accounts and investments through to the less obvious ones like a list of social media passwords. A "letter of wishes "can also be a good idea. In this you can describe who you would like to get the miscellaneous odds and ends. I've seen family feuds start up over who got an old biscuit barrel!

Chapter 4

Divorce or permanent separation – without kids

"One of the hardest things you will ever have to do, my dear, is to grieve the loss of a person who is still alive"

Anonymous

Divorce or permanent separation - without kids

"Will you marry me?" are the words most girls grow up dreaming of hearing from a future prince charming; and I am sure young men are just as anxious about the answer!

BUT we never envision the prospect of getting divorced, even though we know the statistics are roughly one third of first marriages – and two thirds in second marriages - end in divorce. We often think these things only ever happen to other people.

Given the high risk of divorce, what can you do to plan for these eventualities? Let's consider some of the options.

Prenuptial Agreement

The term 'Prenuptial Agreement' frequently appears in the media, particularly in news about celebrity marriages, either when the agreement is made or when celebrities get divorced. A prenuptial agreement, however, is not just reserved for celebrities with millions in assets. In Australia prenuptial agreements are often prepared for anyone wanting to protect their assets where they have unequal wealth upon entering a marriage.

What is a Prenuptial Agreement?

A prenuptial agreement is known in Australia as a Binding Financial Agreement (BFA). It is made before marriage and it can be a useful way to protect spouses' assets. If such an agreement is in place, in the event of separation, stipulated assets in the agreement may be excluded from the spouses' collective property pool (provided that the agreement has been drafted correctly).

Should I get a Prenuptial Agreement?

Prenuptial Agreements are particularly useful for those who have significantly more assets than their partner, or children from prior relationships, as it outlines how the assets should be distributed in the event of a relationship breakdown. It is also advisable to discuss with an independent financial advisor the costs of raising children from prior relationships as this can often be a major cause of marital friction.

It is completely up to an individual to decide whether to make such an agreement and may make property settlements at the end of a marriage less complicated by simply communicating expectations.

How do I get a Prenuptial Agreement?

If you are considering making a prenuptial agreement, make sure it is done correctly as recent cases have shown that legal 'slip-ups' are not looked upon favourably by the Court and may result in an agreement being set aside. If this should happen assets are then open to being distributed as the Court sees fit.

The legal requirements for making a valid prenuptial agreement are strict, and specialist family law advice should be sought. The following steps are essential in making a binding agreement:

- each party must receive independent legal advice;
- the legal advice must be from a lawyer in the Australian jurisdiction (this may be obvious but there have been some cases where agreements have been set aside because legal advice was received from a lawyer practising in another country);
- the agreement must be in writing;
- it should be drafted and signed in the presence of a lawyer, and
- it must contain a complete disclosure of assets, liabilities, expenditure and income.

Two possible problems can arise in the preparation of a prenuptial agreement: one is non-disclosure and the other is unreasonable pressure (duress). Great care should be taken that neither of these occur, if they do then it can be a basis for the setting aside of the agreement.

A recent High Court case Thorne v Kennedy has allowed an appeal against a decision of the Full Family Court on the enforceability of binding financial agreements before and after marriage. Given the decision sets aside the prenuptial agreement it is hard to imagine that most of the existing agreements will survive this test. prenuptial agreements are by their nature tilted against the poorer partner with the emotional pressure attached of "sign this or we won't get married"

> "The wife, then aged 36 and the husband, then aged 67 met over the internet in mid- 2006. At the time that they met, the wife was not living in the country of her birth and her English language skills had been informally acquired. She had no children and no assets of any substance. The husband however was an Australian property developer with assets worth at least $18 million. He was divorced from his first wife, and had adult children." http://www.hcourt.gov.au/assets/cases/02-Brisbane/b14-2017/Thorne_SP.pdf

Whilst a lay person might consider that 'she married him for his money', a useful exercise in understanding the current divorce system is to read the case notes. It is also why I am excited by the prospect of technology disrupting the legal profession. By way of reference at the pontification that occurs take for example this paragraph: -

> "Well, is there a need for braces when there is a belt? No, but I rely on it in addition to it because, in my respectful submission, it goes to the history of the law of equity and it goes to which way the courts are going to go. Is this brave new world to be characterised by the courts retreating from equity or by the courts being particularly alert to the equitable problems likely to arise once freedom in the marketplace enables the rich to gain control over the not so rich? http://www.hcourt.gov.au/cases/case_b14-2017

I do hope this 'brave new world' starts to apply common sense and plain English to breakdowns in personal relationships that need simple and timely solutions.

Marriage Insurance

A colleague once told me of a great idea that she and her husband had - "marriage insurance"

This was basically seeing a counsellor BEFORE they needed help with issues in their marriage. It was used as a pre-emptive tool to help keep communication honest and open between them.

Once a month they sat down with a counsellor, so they could openly communicate knowing they were in an environment where if they were unable to articulate clearly, the counsellor would be able to help facilitate mutual understanding.

Communicate don't Cheat

If your marriage is breaking down and you are starting to consider activities outside of the agreed boundaries of your relationship – DON'T!

One of the worst things you can do to your spouse other than domestic physical or verbal abuse (which is outside the scope of this book) is to betray their trust.

If you want to have a higher chance of an amicable divorce, 'don't get caught with your pants down'. Simple really.

By communicating prior to crossing agreed relationship boundaries, you substantially reduce the risk of a high conflict (and expensive) divorce.

Understand the Divorce process

While the divorce process is different for everyone, it typically involves the following steps:

1. Notification by one party they don't wish to remain in the marriage or de facto relationship

2. Counselling
3. Financial Settlement and Parenting Orders prepared, agreed and lodged
4. Physical Separation – for a minimum of one year in Australia
5. Divorce Application granted

How you go about these steps can vary between couples based on personality, anger, finance position and legal representation (more information is provided in the next chapter).

Divorce Lawyers

As with any profession: you have good ones and bad ones. Many people seek referrals from friends or colleagues who have divorced, use an internet search engine, or ask the Family Court.

I would also recommend going to a Family Court and having the process explained by the court administrators. Or if you want to be serious about Planning Plan B for divorce, spend a day in a family court room before you get married and hear what can happen after the wedding day. Then share a date night communicating about what you learned and discuss the 'what if?' scenarios.

Divorce Amicably

As Artificial Intelligence (AI) is being developed, the future will hopefully see amicable divorces increase. Two businesses stand out, though neither is in Australia – YET.

https://thistoo.co/

https://amicable.io/

AI and machine learning will search through family law court cases and find similar precedents and provide you with the likely court outcome of a financial percentage between spouses.

Alternatively, divorce mediators can reduce the length of time, and therefore cost, as compared to going through a lengthy and expensive court process.

Based on personal experience though, an amicable divorce can only occur between two rational people; so, make sure you are not the cheating spouse as there is a higher risk you'll also have an irrational spouse.

Getting Divorced

According to the Australian Bureau of Statistics, in Australia, there are around 50,000 divorces each year. There are many nuances when it comes to handling financial decisions after a divorce or separation and I recommend you seek advice for your personal circumstances in the unlikely event Divorce does occur in your life.

Divorce or permanent separation – without kids

Do you have the following documentation?	Yes or No	Action to take	By when?
Agreed asset allocation and worst case scenario plan			
Prenuptial Agreement (if not likely to be under duress)			
Information on the joint family assets and income			
Contact details – lawyer, mediator,			
Information for useful organisations			
Marriage certificate			
Birth certificate			
Binding Nominations			
Financial position at date of marriage			

Key take-away:

Divorce is almost always a very messy business even when children are not involved. Marriages sometimes come to a foreseeable end, when both parties identify that continuing is somewhat pointless. However, they often come to an end after an acrimonious break-up. Either way, it's best to know what to do if either should occur.

10 Questions for an Expert

Family Lawyer Melinda Winning from Barkus Doolan

1) **What documents would I need to prepare to get divorced and how long does it take to prepare them?**

   A divorce Application can be filed 12 months after the date of final separation. The Application is reasonably straightforward and would only take an hour or so to prepare. After the date of filing it will be determined somewhere between 6 weeks and 3 months in the Sydney Registry. It will not usually be listed within six weeks as you must provide the Application has been served one month before the divorce hearing if it is not a joint Application for divorce. If there are no children of the marriage under 18 years, there is no need for an attendance at Court if the divorce is not contested (i.e. the other party has not filed a Response). A joint Application for divorce is a good option if it is amicable and that way you can share the filing fee and there will be no issues with service.

2) **Would I able to prepare these documents myself online and if so how would I do this?**

   Possibly, but it is always better to get advice from a lawyer as you need to prove service and make sure all jurisdictional grounds are satisfied. You also need to be aware that a divorce will set in place a 12-month limitation period within which you have to sort out your financial and property matters. You can go online and fill out the Application electronically on the Family Court website www.familycourt.gov.au.

3) **Do we have to get a lawyer each and what other options are there to negotiate a separation?**

   You cannot use one lawyer – you will each need your own lawyer although it is not compulsory for each party to obtain independent legal advice. It is always preferable for both parties to obtain legal advice as it mitigates the possibility of one party attempting to undo the agreement and assists in ensuring the consent Orders are made by the Court. In parenting matters, Family Dispute Resolution is a good way to try and resolve any issues. You can also attend private mediation with several government funded service providers such as Unifam and Relationships Australia. Legally assisted mediation (where both parties have lawyers present) is also a useful tool if you are both legally represented.

4) **What financial obligations do I have if we own a house together, but my ex is living there while I rent somewhere waiting to sell it?**

It depends upon the nature of the loan secured against the property as to whether you are liable. Usually, the party with exclusive use and occupation of the home will pay the outgoings on it whilst they live there but this depends upon the parties' respective incomes and capacity to make those payments. It may be possible where one party is employed, and the other is not to apply for spouse maintenance to fund the loan repayments and other outgoings.

5) **We have a pet we both love, how do the courts decide who gets our dog?**

Pets are treated as property – there is no uniform approach. The Court will therefore look at whose name the pet is registered in, who wants the pet, reasons for wanting it, capacity to maintain it and whether it has any value (in dollar terms). The best way to resolve issues around pets is by agreement as there is no way to predict what a court would do.

6) **If my ex has an accident and can't work a year after we split up do I have an obligation to help them?**

You may be liable for spouse maintenance if you have the capacity to meet some of their expenses. This will be payable whilst ever the other non-working spouse can establish that they do not have the capacity to earn an income.

7) **What if I sponsored them to become an Australian citizen, does this mean they have to go back to their original country?**

Not necessarily but it certainly can be the case that separation and/or divorce can impact upon a party's ability to remain in this country. It depends on the type of visa they are on here in Australia – advice from an immigration lawyer is essential.

8) **My ex is being abusive what options do I have to prevent them coming near me?**

If someone has been subjected to abuse and family violence (which doesn't have to be physical or explicit but can also involve stalking, harassment and intimidation) they may apply for an Apprehended Violence Order in NSW.

9) **I run my own business, so all my assets are in my spouse's name, how does this impact the financial split?**

In most cases all the assets held in the names of both parties comprise the matrimonial pool of assets. However, how property is held (that is, its' legal ownership) may impact upon the outcome of the proceedings and importantly the Court's approach to make a property adjustment Order.

10) **What is the best way to leave a relationship in your experience so as to avoid the divorce courts? i.e. are there any pre-indicators something will turn toxic given all your years of experience and knowledge**

Try to separate in counselling with a trusted third-party present – if you sense things are going downhill in a relationship seek legal advice from an experienced Family Law practitioner so you have a plan in place in the event of separation and know what to expect. You do not want to be taken by surprise or put your head in the sand, these are the cases where things go badly for one party, usually the one who is the least prepared!

Chapter 5

Divorce or permanent separation – with kids

"When there are kids involved, there's no such thing as divorce."

Carl Whitaker

Divorce or permanent separation - with kids

A divorce without children is a complicated matter and inevitably delivers turmoil to both partners. The presumption in this chapter is that you have read the preceding chapter on Divorce or permanent separation – without kids.

A divorce *with* children – especially minor children - is a minefield, juggling concerns of immediate emotional needs as well as the long-term welfare of the children.

Even the most amicable divorces have moments of extreme stress and if you had different parental styles and values causing friction whilst you were together, then be prepared for further angst now you are parenting in a manner that no longer involves compromise.

Telling the kids

One of the first questions that will be raised is how to tell the children. This is particularly hard if you are not the one to instigate the split. How you prepare to do this isn't something you are likely to pre-plan but no doubt you will have advice from a counsellor or through reading online as to how to best approach this difficult conversation.

It's often helpful for divorcing parents to come up with a plan and present it to their children together, while always keeping the lines of communication open. Kids benefit from having honest, age appropriate conversations about the changes their family is experiencing.

That said, sudden change can be hard on children. If appropriate, give them a few weeks' notice before moving them to a new home, or before one spouse moves out. It can be helpful to minimise changes as much as possible in the months and years following a divorce. However financial realities may not make this possible - keeping things similar in furnishings and surroundings was something that helped my children. They also keep a photo of our family before the divorce in their room.

Parenting Arrangements

Children have less mental health issues when they maintain close contact with both parents. Research suggests that kids who have a poor relationship with one or both parents may have a harder time dealing with family upheaval and their own relationships as adults. Below are three types of parenting relationships following a relationship breakdown.

1. Co Parenting Amicably

Life is less complicated in making decisions concerning your children when you can co parent amicably. Should you be able to reach an agreement it is advised to have this reviewed by a family lawyer however it is not a mandatory requirement in obtaining parenting orders.

The Family Court of Australia website www.familycourt.gov.au is regularly updated and it is recommended to use this resource to assist in drafting a parenting plan and consent orders.

What is a parenting plan?

A parenting plan is a written agreement that sets out parenting arrangements for child/ren. The plan is worked out and agreed jointly, you and your former partner do not need to go to court.

Unless a court orders otherwise, you and your former partner can agree to change a parenting order by entering a parenting plan.

A parenting plan is not a legally enforceable agreement. It is different from a parenting order, which is made by a court.

For more information, see the Parenting Plan information on Family Relationships online.

http://www.familyrelationships.gov.au/BrochuresandPublications/Pages/parenting-plans.aspx

What are consent orders?

A consent order is a written agreement that is approved by a court. A consent order can cover parenting arrangements for children as well as financial arrangements such as property and maintenance. Any person concerned with the care, welfare and development of a child can apply for parenting orders.

Consent orders have the same legal effect as if they had been made by a judicial officer after a court hearing. The Court must be satisfied that the orders you ask for are in the best interest of the child.

You can read more about the best interests of a child in the following link:-

http://www.familycourt.gov.au/wps/wcm/connect/fcoaweb/family-law-matters/family-law-in-australia/parenting-cases-the-best-interests-of-the-child

For step-by-step details on how to file consent orders, see the following information:

- Applying to the court for orders fact sheet - http://www.familycourt.gov.au/wps/wcm/connect/fcoaweb/reports-and-publications/publications/court-orders/applying-to-the-court-for-orders
- How do I – Apply for consent orders - http://www.familycourt.gov.au/wps/wcm/connect/fcoaweb/how-do-i/apps-orders/consent-orders/applying-consent-orders

I completed our parenting plan and consent orders using the links above with discussions from my children's father and despite them coming back from the Court a few times for adjustment we got them through without the need for spending thousands in legal fees. I had a one-hour meeting with a great lawyer from Barkus Doolan who helped answer my questions and made some suggested changes and then I lodged them personally with the Family Court. Clients and friends however have not been so fortunate with hundreds of thousands in legal fees and years of uncertainty ensuring an amicable co-parenting relationship was not a viable option.

2. *Sole Custody*

Sole custody is where a sole parent has both sole parental responsibility to make all the decisions impacting the child(ren) without having to consult the other parent *and* the child(ren) live with one parent only.

The court will grant sole parental responsibility if it is in the children's best interests. The most obvious cases are where one parent lacks mental capacity because of, for example, a mental illness. Another is where the parent is incarcerated, or where there is evidence of the parent making decisions that put the children at risk of harm, e.g. repeated driving under the influence of drugs or alcohol, or exposing the children to violence or physical or psychological harm.

In these circumstances even where a parent has abandoned their child/ren it is advised to seek the advice of a family lawyer.

3. *Parallel Parenting*

Co-parenting amicably depends on two rational parents putting their children's needs first though, given the back log of Family Law cases, unfortunately this rarely happens. It is incredibly difficult to see children being subjected to this form of emotional abuse; whilst research has been conducted on long term detrimental effects, there is currently nothing to prevent this from occurring.

If a high conflict separation has occurred then the reality is co-parenting is often not an option, as trying to agree on parenting decisions is just not possible. In these situations, parallel parenting provides minimal contact between the parents to minimise any potential for conflict. Parallel parenting with low contact between conflicting parents is preferable to shared parenting between parents who simply cannot agree.

In this situation, the parenting plan and consent orders should be as detailed and specific as possible to provide for clear guidelines and expectations. Whilst this reduces flexibility and communication between what goes on in the 'other' home it is better than maintaining an emotionally negative relationship for all concerned.

Potential areas for conflict include the following: -

Diet - Where one parent likes convenience food and the other likes homemade, organic meals. The courts or mediators won't enter into this level of detail. If you are the amazing organic chef, then be prepared to accept that the kids are eating food with their other parent that you'd prefer they don't consume.

Religion – Do you both agree on the religion in which you want your children to be raised? If you want them to go to a religious school, will you both endeavour to meet the commitments involved on the weekends that you have the children?

Education – What schooling system would you both like for you children and in the event of a split who is going to pay and in what proportions? Regarding school trips, excursions or overseas tours, who will be responsible for the payment?

Holiday locations – Are there countries that one parent considers dangerous, and if so how will you agree on holiday travel? Travel overseas provides so many benefits to children such as knowledge of history, language, culture and geography. And yet *both* parents need to agree to have the children leave the country. If one doesn't agree for reasons of, say, jealously, then barring the cost of a court case, the kids are the ones who miss out on these experiences.

Discipline – What kind of discipline do you believe is appropriate? Children are adaptable and so will quickly learn whether they can play the parents off against each other or whether you still show a united front. Raising children is different for everyone. My view is I want my children to be ethical, moral, educated, polite and happy adults who contribute to the world. This has never meant they get away with rudeness at any age. I am fortunate that my ex agrees and to this day they know if they get in trouble at one parent's house, the other person will know and back that punishment. In fact, the biggest complaint they have is that they get joint birthday and Christmas presents still!

Having seen a parallel parenting arrangement where there is absolutely no discipline at the mother's home, it is then also difficult to instigate in the father's home. But good manners are consistently encouraged, and I am sure over time children will learn the benefits of polite behaviour.

Risk and safety – Is one parent adventurous and one conservative? How will you decide on activities for the children such as motor bike riding, skiing, sky diving etc? Do you agree to disagree, compromise, and educate the children or accept you can't control what happens in the other parent's care?

Activities – What activities will your children take on outside school? Regarding the logistics and payment, who will take them to the activities and how will payment be agreed upon?

Technology – At what age do you agree your children should be on digital tablets and mobile phones? How will these devices be paid for … and by whom?

Social media – At what age do you agree for your children to use social media applications such as Facebook, Snapchat and Instagram?

Other family members – Are there any family members or friends about whom you feel concerned with your children being in their care?

Public transport – At what age are you both comfortable that is safe for your children to travel alone on public transport? This includes bus, train, taxi and Uber. Do you agree to obtain public transport cards outside a travel zone even if you don't see your child at your out of zone residence?

Introducing new partners – Do you have an agreed time frame you should be seeing a new partner before introducing them to your children. What about social media posts of your new partner with the children? What about a new partner's children? There is a whole book that can be written on the do's and don'ts here unfortunately though new love isn't always rational!

Clothing and personal items – Are clothing and personal effects those of the child and are free to go with them between houses or are they linked to the respective homes and so, effectively, they have two sets?

Personal grooming – Expenses, especially for teenage girls, can vary in terms of "necessity" To have the discussion around waxing, haircuts, ear piercing, laser hair removal are topics that can be fraught with issues as to who pays and at what age.

Medical – With young children, if something happens to one parent, the other will generally need to step into help. So, in my experience, this has been the hardest one to deal with. For all intents and purposes, we remain a "family", dependent on each other in the event of a medical emergency where one of the parents is not able to look after a sick child.

However, there are important tax, family benefit considerations that need to be taken into consideration, if you are separated. Who will pay the private medical insurance and who can make a claim on behalf of the children.

Consider a separate Medicare card for each parent with the dependants listed, relevant hospital cover and the need to discuss who pays for the children's cover, together with care logistics in the event they are unwell and not able to attend day care or school.

Dental – the need for dental alignment in young teens is one which should be agreed upon. Most families make this decision based on the capacity to pay and the degree of aesthetic need vs actual dental issues that are being resolved between parents. Unfortunately, in a high conflict parenting situation, this can become yet another battle ground.

Bed time – Unfortunately until you experience getting children to sleep you can never imagine how much of a drama it can become. Some try meditation, music, a book, comforter, (or lay there until they get to sleep), co-sleeping, and other methods involving 'threat or bribery'.

If you disagree on the when and how of bed time while you are together, then the extremes of your views will creep in when you are co-parenting.

I hear many stories of children coming home from the other parent's tired and cranky because they were allowed to put themselves to sleep.

In an amicable co-parenting arrangement, this could be discussed with a view to getting them to sleep sooner.

In a high conflict parenting arrangement, this is simply another way of antagonising each other.

Unfortunately, you can't control what happens at the other parent's home, so just do the best you can when they are in your care and encourage them to set their own sleep routines for implementing at both parents' homes.

Conception or adoption information – given children are now often conceived with the assistance with advances in science, how do you agree on letting the children know. Was there IVF, a surrogate donor or other means of conception that occurred that whilst at the time was agreed but in the event of an acrimonious split left waiting explosively in the side lines ready to blow a child's self-belief apart?

Sex education – Schools prepare children in some areas; however, unless you are having conversations with your children before this time frame you may find the topics discussed in one home before you are ready in your own.

Change over procedures – Parents who co-parent amicably will just make arrangements that over time start to get into a new routine that works best for the children. They may include dropping off bags of clothes and personal items for the children, access to a home or garage to drop items, picking up from school or day care or many other configurations that fit in with your day to day living arrangements.

Parents in a high conflict divorce find the changeover procedure can become another interaction that is just used to try and hurt an ex-partner.

I have heard of the following procedures:

1. Meeting in a McDonalds car park
2. Texting from one end of a train station to someone on the other side while the children walk out unattended as the parents can't stand the sight of each other
3. Having children take their clothes and shoes off at the door way before going to the other parent's home (surely a form of emotional abuse)
4. Parents being the ones to move out and leaving the kids in the family home

Communication – When I was newly separated, I received some advice from a dear friend who died of cancer in the last couple of years. He sat down with his ex-wife and they agreed on a piece of paper how they would raise their only son. And that is what they adhered to. The mother had him during the working week and the father on weekends. This was so he could take him to compulsory school sports and spend a Sunday enjoying quality time. This worked for their family.

My ex and I communicate regularly, the kids know if they get into trouble with one of us the other parent will know and back up the other parent. That consistency is maintained but it was made easier because we had very similar parenting styles and values to begin with.

Should you have vastly different values when you are married, and ideas around parenting, then those differences become amplified when divorced. When you are together you try and reach 'middle ground'; when you separate, you may go to the extremes because the truth is, you can; you are no longer in a relationship with your ex.

Yet your children are. And you need to always think about them first. If this is hard at first, especially if you have been cheated on, it will be a case of fake it until you make it. One day you will communicate with little emotional attachment and over time apparently, you may even become friends.

However, should communication not be an option, consider the many software applications available, or an old-fashioned text book, in which you record information that is necessary for the care of the children.

Living locations – given the separation of your financial assets, you may find circumstances change either around affordability or employment opportunities, whereby one or both of you want to change location. Courts can make orders in terms of a parent with the most custody not being able to move outside a certain distance. Given the huge potential for conflict it is best to firstly talk any potential move through with your co-parent where this is possible. If communication has totally broken down, seek legal advice.

Financial Arrangements

Your personal income and asset levels will largely determine the financial arrangements you will reach in raising your children together as co parents. Being open and transparent about your finances as a family whilst together will help enormously in the event you do divorce.

Should one spouse believe the other is hiding assets or income as they were of the opinion during the marriage they were better off financially than in fact they were, this will cause conflict.

Should you be in dispute in regard to child maintenance it is recommended to contact Department of Human Services for advice and assistance whilst waiting on the court orders.

Do you have the following documentation?	Yes or No	Action to take	By when?
Agreed asset allocation and worst case scenario plan			
Prenuptial Agreement (if not likely to be under duress)			
Information on the joint family assets and income			
Agreement on parenting style, religion and education			

Key take-away:

When children are involved, addressing divorce issues can be like walking a tightrope – best to tread very carefully and to have a plan 'to get to the other side' of the many issues involved. Professional input may be invaluable in more ways than one.

10 Questions for an Expert

Family Lawyer Melinda Winning from Barkus Doolan

1) **Am I able to take my children overseas without the other parent needing to know for a holiday or family visit? If no how do I get approval where it is for valid urgent family reasons?**

   Not if there are proceedings on foot or if there are any Orders in place – if either of these things apply you will need the written consent of the other parent and this needs to be by way of a statutory declaration.

2) **Do I have to continue to pay spousal maintenance if my ex remarries?**

   Spouse maintenance will end upon your former spouse re-marrying.

3) **If we can't agree to co parent what are our other options as I no longer want to communicate at all with my ex?**

   If shared parenting or equal time is to succeed, you need excellent communication. If this is not there, you will be looking at an arrangement that involves significant or substantial time which usually looks like alternate weekends and possibly a night or afternoon during the school week, subject of course to the ages of the children and there being no risk factors or family violence.

4) **How do we make decisions on schooling and activities for our children if we disagree on everything?**

   Family therapy or counselling may assist – some people meet with counsellors every term or so to try and agree on such matters. If these matters are not the subject of agreement the Court will have to decide.

5) **What is parental alienation and how do I prevent this occurring if it looks like I will be the one instigating the leaving of our relationship?**

   This involves one parent undermining and devaluing the other parent to such an extent (by words or actions or both) that the children become aligned with that parent and may then be reluctant to have relationship with the other parent. This may ultimately result in the children having no relationship with the alienated parent. There is no way to prevent this, but keep your eyes and ears open and make sure any initial signs of this are stomped on early. Don't let it get to the point of no return.

6) **Have you heard of a couple that were able to maintain an amicable relationship for the sake of the children and how did they achieve this outcome whilst going through the court process?**

   The court process and litigation are very destructive. Family therapy and counselling is a good place to start. And always focus on the kids, because if that is genuinely the priority for both parties they can often continue their relationship as parents.

7) **Am I able to prepare my legal documentation without a lawyer if we both agree on custody?**

   Yes, but legal advice is always recommended (and not because I am a lawyer!)

8) **What should I do to prevent my ex-spouse not paying child maintenance or the agreed shared amount of the children's expenses?**

   You will need an Assessment to issue and you can ask for this by calling the Department of Human Services (Child Support).

You can then ask the Department to collect on your behalf. For an Agreement to be enforceable you will need Binding Child Support agreement (you will need a lawyer to prepare and advise on this document for it to be binding).

9) **I absolutely hate my ex, but I know I need to communicate with them as our children are only minors. Is there any way to do this without having to email or call them?**

There are several Apps now for divorced parents to communicate, but it is better to have a record of all communication, so texts and emails are not a bad idea. Remember they can be used as evidence so keep all communications cordial and business like – put the hate to one side and focus on the kids.

10) **Emotionally, I find it hard around family holidays to not be in the company of my children as the split was not my decision. How do I come to accept the current situation so that I am not depressed on these occasions? i.e. are there any good counselling books things you have seen people implement that help not end up in such a high conflict situation**

Counselling is an excellent way forward. You will need to come up with strategies to cope with those difficult times which can be lonely following divorce.

Wisdom from an Expert Philipa Thornton Executive Director of the Resource Therapy Institute of Australia

Family breakup, separation or divorce is difficult for everyone. There's grief for all in this situation and it's when we need to be helping our children the most. It is most difficult for a child, who has no say in what is happening. It can have negative consequences, such that our children are at risk of poor school performance, dropping out of school earlier, behavioural issues, anxiety and depression. These risks are increased if there is antagonism between parents and if one parent speaks negatively about the other around the children. The good news is that if parents are supportive, most children do not have these problems.

Good ideas to support your child cope with family break up:

- Keep to your usual routine as much as possible – bed times, school runs etc.
- Maintain a respectful relationship with your co parent, as the father or mother of your children
- Help your child keep in touch with both parents (Providing there are no child safety risks)
- It is advised generally for children under 4 to avoid overnight separations from the main carer. Follow your child's cues as to where they feel comfortable
- Don't argue in front of your child; save difficult topics for when you can discuss them in private.
- Don't be disparaging of your co-parent with negative comments or body language. Remember your children are 50% you and 50% your co-parent. When they hear negative comments, they can take this to heart.
- It's natural for a child to be distressed and angry sometimes. Take care to listen to ensure they feel comfortable and understood. Allow expression of feelings. Sometimes children will

regress to younger behaviour for a time and may need more nurturing.

- Reassure your continued loving care and parenting will continue. If they are older, make sure they know the breakup is not their fault.
- Put your child's needs above your own hurt, anxiety or angry feelings. Attend to your own self-care and need for support, by reaching out and connecting with your social networks or a counsellor.

https://www.aaimhi.org/ for more information on infant mental health. For older children see parenting and child health at www.cyh.com

Self-help suggestions to help you feel better. 5 preventive measures you can take to reduce the likelihood of mental illness occurring

1. *Find your tribe.*

    There are a wide variety of therapeutic modalities available, aside from medications, which have been shown to be effective in addressing mental health issues. Traditional talk therapies, body oriented approaches, (such as mindfulness, relaxation training etc.), and exercise/lifestyle approaches, are all part of a solid and effective, non-medication based approach, to ameliorating mental health problems.

It is well known that social connections are crucial for a person who is experiencing depression. Social isolation is one of the hallmarks of a depressed person as they withdraw from social connections. An Australian study's findings (Cruwy's et al., 2014) demonstrate that those who not only joined a local group (some did yoga, art, sports or sewing) but also identified with their group, had lower depression scores after three months' follow-up.

Professor Alexander Haslam (Cruwy's et al., 2014), a co-author, said:

> *We were able to find clear evidence that joining groups, and coming to identify with them, can alleviate depression. "Our work shows that the 'group' aspect of social interaction is critical ... a group has to matter psychologically to be beneficial for depression – simply "showing up" without commitment or engagement is unlikely to be sufficient.*

The authors conclude that their study suggests…

> *…that tackling the challenge of depression involves not just putting the person back into the group, but also putting the group back into the person.*

It seems finding your tribe, mob or community is important to healing depression. It's vital this group is a place where you can feel a connection. It could be taking up a hobby, acting classes, Yoga, community classes, Laughter Yoga, dancing, sports, it could even be online.

I was on a talkback radio show for ABC 702 with Radio host Philip Clarke and Professor Katina Michael from the University of Wollongong, where we were pondering is 'Facebook making us sad.' A lady called in and said Facebook had helped her recover from depression and its isolation. She told us that when a relative put up a profile for her, at first, she was unnerved but as she found her friends and family coming out to support her she felt connected. How wonderful.

So, find your support network to gain connection and healing in the long term. We all need a cheer squad at times to send us love, validation and affirmation.

2. *The power of pets*

Another other option is to start up your own tribe. I had a car accident where I was rear ended, leading to an injury and my beautiful car being written off. Very sad loss of course. Certainly, an unexpected and tough break, to say the least! This event turned out to be a turning point in my life. My days spent on the bus travelling 90 minutes each way to go to work got rather tedious. I decided to go full time in my private practice Marriage Works, and have never looked back.

Another light that shone at this time was a friend suggesting I get a pet, which I did. Taneisha (a cat) was 12 years of age when she came to live with me from a breeder. She was well loved but ready to retire as she could no longer have kittens. I joke: I rescued her from sex slavery – she was a champion Burmese breeding feline. I always had animals for most of my young life, raising lambs, fish, chickens, budgies, a duck and cats.

Taneisha is a beautiful chocolate Burmese (low allergy too!) and spectacularly loving. She has a sixth sense for knowing when a person is down or upset. One day, I was seeing a family member and was surprised when my cat went straight up to a girl who was agitated and upset … and jumped up into her lap. Naturally the child started to stroke her as she gradually settled down. Taneisha did a lot to help soothe her.

Pets such as dogs, cats, birds - or any animal you personally connect with - can become a wonderful and devoted part your life. The benefits are profound. The unconditional loving of an animal cannot be overestimated. I have seen people care for their pets so tenderly, taking them for walks, feeding, talking to and cuddling them – all incredibly healing for anyone.

There is scientific evidence from studies of therapy animals visiting nursing homes; hospital units and so forth are helping to heal and bringing cheer to all. Only the other day I heard the 'baa' of a goat. Now I live in metropolitan Sydney, so this is an unusual sound to hear when it's not coming from the TV. None of my neighbours has a goat in their yard. I look across my balcony to see the 'baaing' was coming from the nursing home across the road. Evidently there was a petting zoo there for residents to touch and physically connect. What joy I felt as I could see the residents outside in the fresh air enjoying their interactions.

3. *You are what you eat.*

It is long known that a healthy diet plays an important part in a person's overall well-being and ability to handle stress. In a large study of 15,093 people who were followed over 10 years, the traditional Mediterranean diet, which includes eating nuts, fruits and vegetables, legumes, fish/seafood, cereals, and monounsaturated oils, had a protective effect and lowered the risk of depression (Sánchez-Villegas et al., 2015). There is a body of thinking from scientists that depression could be partly due to a lack of essential nutrients. There is an added benefit to eating healthily: food is fuel, and if we fill our 'tank' with nutrient-rich and healthy foods, our system is likely to feel the benefits. This is something we can control in our lives. Luckily fresh vegetables are relatively cheap and easy to come by.

There is also tentative research into the role inflammation may play in depression. https://www.healthyplace.com/other-info/mental-health-newsletter/could-depression-be-caused-by-inflammation-in-the-body/ so review you're eating and plan for a healthy start.

4. *Movement Counts*

Now to our bodies. We are movement machines and much research has been done to demonstrate the effectiveness of exercise on our mind and our bodies. We release endorphins, which are neurotransmitters and powerful brain chemicals, to lower stress. Research also suggests that the benefits of exercise may be long lasting. Depressed adults who took part in a fitness program displayed significant improvements over depression, anxiety, and self-esteem (Craft and Perna, 2004)

The endorphins are our body's natural pain relief substances and provide positive feelings, like those given by morphine. Perhaps you have heard of the 'runner's high' where a person feels euphoric and energised after a workout. (Craft and Perna, 2004)

Exercise has many positive benefits these include

- Lowering stress
- Improving self- esteem
- Reducing anxiety
- Depression relief
- Better sleeping
- Improves heart health
- Boosts energy levels
- Lowers blood pressure
- Increases strengthen and tones muscles
- Strengthens bones
- Helps reduce fat

And it is *free*. Start small at first. A walk around the block is a beginning, and then progressively add a bit more. Great if you can access a park or a nature reserve. There is something special about being in nature for us humans. Get your green on. The beach is another wonderful place; take a dip in the ocean and get your dose of positive ions for free. I find there is something very cleansing and incredibly healing about being in water.

5. *Nourish your Spirit*

Today in Australia and most of the western world we live in a highly materialistic world, overflowing with technology. The pressure to compete and maintain expensive lifestyles may be draining our spirit. It is thought that a sense of spiritual impoverishment is a contributor in modern societies ever increasing epidemic of depression and anxiety. Perhaps we are undernourished spiritually, leading us to feel a deeper sense of dissatisfaction, disconnection and distress.

In talking about spirituality, I am referring to the belief system that informs and guides your life towards its highest good. Spirituality is uniquely personal and can be connected to nature, animals or those beliefs espoused by organized religions. Faith can be very healing. Perhaps you grew up in a religious system – Judaism, Buddhism, Catholicism, Islam or Hinduism to name a few. You may want to revisit your local church, synagogue, temple or mosque to reconnect.

If this isn't your thing, you can find spiritual support in many forms. Music offers many people relief and has long been available for spiritual nurturance.

Joining a choir offers a powerful spiritual expression, support of a group and brain growth. It's hard to be unhappy for long at a sing-along. I enjoy Salsa as a dance and the music is cheerful and uplifting. I have a Buddhist friend who loves singing in an Anglican choir, so there are many possibilities.

Songs are often intimate and celebratory, offering you harmony (sorry for the pun). Singing lifts your spirits in all senses emotionally and physically. Your brain releases endorphins and oxytocin, powerful mood enhancers and it alleviates stress. Music is soul food.

6. *The Power of the Pen.*

Writing a journal, whether on paper or digitally, has been a form of catharsis for centuries. There is something incredibly potent in putting pen to paper that aids in release and reflection. Oprah swears by a daily gratitude list as a supportive practice. Affirmations can be amazingly influential especially when written. I especially like Sondra Ray's books how to write affirmations, although slightly dated, as they are from the 1970's. Think about it, our negative thoughts are merely negative affirmations we repeat. What if we were to swap them out for good? I particularly like Emile Coue's simple affirmative sentence – "*Every day in every way I am getting better and better.*" Write and say it out loud and with conviction 20 times a day for 31 days for an experiment. Let us know how it works.

Many a novel takes us on a journey of enquiry, curiosity and fulfilment. For some it may be the Bible or Kabala, or something in a fictional book we can connect with. A personal heroine of mine is Rachel Naomi Remen; her books are full of stories that heal (see Resources). I also enjoy a fantasy novel occasionally, as usually it involves the underdog rising and completing a quest, involving their personal growth and triumph for the good guys.

We are so lucky to have access to the written word, whether it is on paper or in our kindle; your local library is full of them, so join up for free. While there you might even look around for a book club to join and discuss the emotional journey an author has taken you on.

Personal blogs are like online diaries, which offer a form of connection. There are blogs on every interest out there – cooking, parenting, fitness, fishing, you name it. Often people can authentically share their perils and success in an honest and intimate manner. Google and find your online community.

7. Meditation

Naturally I must mention meditation as a means of spiritual nourishment. Eastern traditions have been using meditation for many centuries both sitting still and in the form of movement. Mindfulness meditation has been taken up by mental health professionals. You can find many groups, self-help books and online forums, to access mindful meditation. (See the resources section).

Yoga, Tai Chi and martial arts offer some form of spiritual practice to explore, as well as the added benefit of physical movement in a group environment.

If you want to go for 'an intensive' and have 10 days spare, then I would suggest a vipassana retreat. The word vipassana means "to see things as they really are" and help you to a greater self-understanding and reboot your emotions and priorities. I attended the International Centre for Mediation in Morisset, a Buddhist group from the Burmese tradition headed by Mother Sayamagyi in her life. It was both challenging and divine and all for $50 a day with the healthiest and yummiest food. Yoga weekends away can be a wonderful escape and time out from the world.

8. *Touch and Connection*

We are tactile creatures; the touch of massage is supportively intimate with a trusted professional. It can put you in touch with your humanity. Both giving and receiving massage can bring connection and energy to one's spirit. Many of us do not have another to caress or hold us; massage can give you a safe place to feel nurtured.

I hope you found some help and inspiration in reading this. You are certainly not alone and there is help out there. Please have the courage to reach out. I say this with a heavy heart as last week, dear friends of mine lost their son to suicide and are heartbrokenly devastated. With the right help, this too shall pass.

Chapter 6

Disability or incapacity due to accident or illness

"The thing about the Paralympics is, they're not only incredible athletes, but all of them have been through some sort of tragedy, whether it's from an accident, an illness or even a military injury."

Bob Condron

Disability or incapacity due to accident or illness

Very few of us would be in a financial position to take leave from work at the best of times, never mind when income drops due to an inability to work whilst medical expenses mount.

How can you protect yourself against loss of income and the strain of medical bills whilst you are medically frail, mentally exhausted and still keeping on top of the normal day to day routines and responsibilities? Below are the main options available for you to consider in compiling your Plan B.

Income Protection Insurance

Income protection insurance replaces your lost income due to injury or sickness. It is an important consideration for anyone who relies on personal services income to cover day to day living expenses. It is especially applicable for self-employed people, those with a large mortgage, small business owners or professionals whose business relies heavily on them as the key contributors to running the enterprise.

Income protection replaces the income you would otherwise personally earn and, accordingly, is often tax deductible. You must however include the amounts received in your tax return – and always seek tax advice specific to your personal circumstances.

Different insurers require different medical information and if you are found to lie on your initial application the policy will be null and void when a potential claim is made. A prime example is the question 'are you a smoker?' Insurance premiums are lower for non-smokers because, actuarially, a non-smoker is less likely to have medical issues.

To calculate how much you should request as cover, determine what your income is either from any or all of these:

- PAYG payment summary,
- Australian Tax Office tax assessment notice,
- Profit and Loss statement,

- Employment contract, or
- An estimate of what your earnings will be.

Also consider the 'excess' and the 'waiting period' options available, both of which will affect the level of premiums and conditions at the time of making a claim. If you have sufficient savings, or annual or long service leave, you may find using these as a buffer will reduce your premiums.

It is also worth noting Income Protection Insurance does not cover loss of employment through redundancy, dismissal or resignation.

Total and Permanent Disability cover

Total and permanent disability (TPD) insurance provides cover if you are totally and permanently disabled. Your insurer will define TPD as when you either:

- Cannot work again in **any** occupation, or
- Cannot work again in your **usual** occupation

TPD insurance may help to cover the costs of rehabilitation, debt repayments and the future cost of living.

Each insurer has different definitions of what is and isn't considered to be totally and permanently disabled. Being off work for a year is NOT 'permanently disabled'.

Generally, an insurance broker will provide a range of options and explain the benefits to you and your circumstances. It is also common for medical questions and a doctor's examination to be requested by the insurer.

Workers Compensation Insurance

Every employer is required by law to cover their employees for injuries or disease that can occur in the workplace or in travelling to and from work.

Any business that employs or hires workers on a full-time, part-time or casual basis, under an oral or written contract of service or apprenticeship, must have workers compensation insurance that covers all its employees regardless of actual payment of wages.

Each State or Territory scheme has different rules in place for domestic employees and, given the cash economy that exists around cleaners and nannies, it is important to ensure that both employer and employees are covered.

If someone employed by you suffers a workplace injury or disease, the workers compensation scheme may provide the injured worker with weekly benefits, medical and hospital expenses, rehabilitation services, certain personal items and a lump sum payment for permanent impairment on the basis set by the scheme. However, given recent changes in the legislation, this does not necessarily cover you for a lifetime of care in the event you are unable to work.

To learn more about workers compensation schemes in Australia visit the website of your state or territory's government agency that is responsible for overseeing the workers compensation and injury management system.

For general information about workers' compensation arrangements across Australia, visit the Safe Work Australia website http://www.safeworkaustralia.gov.au/sites/SWA

New South Wales also provides a government service called Workers Compensation independent review office (WIRO) for assistance with issues with workers compensation claims. https://wiro.nsw.gov.au

Warning: Independent Contractor

Where you are working through an Australian Business Number it is important to be clear on your insurance risk as you may not be covered by Workers Compensation insurance. Check your contract and ask the relevant Human Resources person if you are covered under their insurance policy.

Social Media

We are seeing the rise of social media and its benefits in raising funds for people in need. Sites like the following are all providing assistance in the event an unlikely accident occurs: -

https://au.gofundme.com/

https://mycause.com.au

https://gogetfundraising.com

Obviously, these are a last resort where a Plan B hasn't been put in place and are completely arbitrary. It was only recently shown that the ex-founder of Ksubi was forced to remove his Go Fund me page given the adverse social media reactions, so this really is not so much a plan but an option to consider in the event you didn't create a Plan B.

Community Fundraisers

Local community groups have often been the backbone of assistance in times of need. Whether due to natural disasters, family hardship, or illness, your local network is often the first place to find assistance.

If your community networks are strong, consider their impact on your Planning Plan B for disability or incapacity.

Government Compensation

Should you be injured in a car accident or in an accident where you were not at fault there is usually State based compensation, generally covered as part of compulsory car insurance.

Victims Compensation Scheme

In New South Wales, certain persons affected by criminal offences may apply for an award for compensation for their suffering from the State Government.

While courts may order defendants to pay compensation or "retribution" directly to victims as part of their penalty, they may be unable to meet these high costs, particularly where they have been ordered to serve prison time for an offence.

There may also be significant barriers in claiming compensation from those who commit serious crimes, or domestic and family violence offences.

Victims' compensation schemes exist to offer financial support to victims and their families and to provide some means of redressing the loss, damage or injury suffered because of crimes.

Do you have the following documentation?	Yes or No	Action to take	By when?
Income Protection Insurance			
Total and Permanent Disability Cover			
Are you covered by workers' compensation insurance?			
Contact details – insurer, doctor, etc			

Key take-away

Incapacity, whether temporary or permanent, creates special challenges for the individuals involved as well as those who care for them. Use the links here to research your situation properly

Car Supplies

Car accidents are the highest risk of injury so it is advisable to keep the following items in your vehicle:-

- First aid kit
- Fire extinguisher
- Fire blanket
- Emergency contact details

Story

Lightening does strike twice.

Michael Long is like a cat with nine lives. Leading an envious professional life having been the tour manager of INXS at the height of their success, managing many successful national iconic artists, music festivals and organising the music industry's most illustrious nights the ARIA Awards his life was already more interesting than most.

However, not so enviously he has now been hit twice being almost fatally injured whilst cycling.

In 2012 Michael was in a bunch ride from his home in a suburban Sydney suburb when he almost lost his life. If it were not for the quick thinking of one of his cycling companions, Michael's spine would have been crushed had they moved him resulting in asphyxiation. As it was, he suffered a broken neck and fractured spine resulting in the need to wear a Halo Brace preventing his neck from moving for a period of six months.

Given the periodic nature of Michael's business this meant that he couldn't grow his business and lost opportunities for event management the would have otherwise been able to pursue. However, he was fortunate with the ARIAs being an annual event that the was able to ensure he was rehabilitated sufficiently to continue to perform his role in the 2013 ARIAs.

Almost to the day four years later Michael after much mental challenges was back on the road cycling southbound on Southern Cross Drive in Eastlakes when a truck ran into the back of the bunch, leaving him and another of the riders in hospital with serious injuries.

Michael was riding second to last in the group, which was travelling two abreast. He was chatting with the rider next to him when suddenly he heard the beep of a horn and a sickening crunch.

He was picked up and thrown to the ground, falling hard on his left-hand side. The fall left him with seven broken ribs, a broken collarbone, a punctured lung, a bruised pelvis and a damaged spleen.

As he lay on the ground, he also feared he would be run over.

The Medical Journal of Australia published that between 2007 and 2015, the incidence of hospitalisation for major trauma for because of cycling increased by 8 per cent per year. The total number of cases has doubled over the nine years whilst over the same period there has been a decline in cycling participation. With the Government concerned about the growing health issues with the rise in obesity there are calls to increase funding for safe, connected and well-designed separated roads and paths, better education, reduced speed limits in certain areas and mandatory passing distance across Australia.

10 Questions for an Expert

Insurance expert Mark Sacks from Experien

Disability or incapacity due to accident or illness

1) **What kind of insurance should I have? I don't really do any risky activities, but I am the sole income earner and have two young children?**

    The types of insurance you should consider (beyond health and travel insurance) are:

    - Income protection insurance: pays an ongoing monthly benefit whilst you are unable to work
    - Total and permanent disability (TPD) insurance: pays a lump sum, and
    - Critical illness insurance: pays a lump sum on defined diagnosed medical events such as cancer

    Each person's needs should be individually assessed but a sole income earner with two young children is highly likely to need one or more of the above products. Most claims come from accidents and illnesses that are unrelated to risk activity so the important of having these insurance products is very high.

2) **I was a passenger in a car accident years ago and now my back pain is making it almost impossible to work, is there any means for financial compensation?**

    Yes, there could be via several options. These could include litigation, a claim on CTP insurance and possibly even work cover depending on the circumstances. A lawyer would be best placed to analyse this and provide guidance.

    In addition, it is possible you may be able to claim on any income protection or other insurance you have in place.

3) **I used to take recreational drugs, how does this impact on my insurance?**

This could impact on the ability to get products like income protection. Each insurer has different views on this and some are more lenient than others. Your insurance broker would be best placed to guide you through your personal circumstances.

4) **I have income protection in my superannuation fund, how do I receive this money if I have an accident?**

You would need to first contact the administrator of your super fund. The details of this would be on any recent statement. They in turn will liaise with your trustee and the insurer of the cover who will then guide you through the process on how to claim. It can take longer too process a claim via a superannuation fund compared with if you held that cover directly with an insurer.

5) **How do I keep on top of changes in state based governments?**

In terms of insurance, your broker or insurer can advise you. Plus, you can visit your state treasury/OSR website.

6) **I am living pay check to pay check and can't afford any kind of insurance, how do I protect my family in the event I am injured and unable to work?**

Using preserved superannuation money to pay for your insurance could then be a suitable strategy for you. An insurance broker can help you set this up.

7) **I started smoking after I had income protection insurance in place, do I need to advise anyone and if so who?**

Once a policy is in place, the insurer has already assessed the risk, so you do not need to further inform them of the smoking change, unless you increase your insurance later.

8) **My Father died of cancer at the age of 49 does this impact on my ability to obtain income protection insurance?**

If only the one direct family member (Mum, Dad, Brother or Sister) had the cancer prior to age 60, its unlikely that it will affect your application. If 2 family members have cancer before age 60, then it can affect an application, so best to apply prior to that to be safe.

9) **If I start suffering from depression how do I prove that I am depressed and not just sad? What information will an insurer want to see?**

The insurer will seek medical details from your health care professional/s to confirm the details. They would want to know when it began, the most recent symptoms and treatment and if it impacted ability to work.

10) **Are there any alternatives to protecting against an accident that you are aware of that might be good for people to consider?**

Income Protection and TPD Cover specific to your OWN occupation are generally the most common types of cover to protect you personally for accident. If you run your own business, Business Overheads Insurance should also be considered. It covers your fixed business expenses/overheads if something happens to you and you cannot work but those bills still need to be paid.

Chapter 7

Dismissal from employment

"Failure is the opportunity to begin again more intelligently."
Henry Ford

Dismissal from employment

Unexpected dismissal from employment can arise in several different manners: unfair dismissal, redundancy or an accidental error that resulted in a breach of your employment contract; these can lead to your employment being terminated.

Income Protection Insurance does not cover the loss of income from dismissal from employment - so how can you plan for an unexpected termination of employment?

Unfair dismissal

As the very name implies, there is no way to pre-empt an unfair termination of employment; however, there are general signs that you may want to consider and start planning for a new position if they arise:

1. Poor overall business performance
2. Credit rating of the company is going down so there is financial pressure and they might start looking at quick ways to cut costs
3. Direct management no longer communicating your career development and progression
4. HR issues with other staff who are seen to be favoured by senior management
5. Lack of recognition or promotion
6. A long period of no pay increases
7. Personal circumstances that may be perceived as impacting the business including pregnancy, ill health, and a dependant being unwell.

What records should you keep in the event you are concerned about a potential unfair dismissal?

1. Employment contract
2. Payslips
3. Review and meeting notes or any career development documentation
4. Any warnings received. If they are verbal, ask for them in writing, if it is not received write down your version of events and ask you employer to sign them as accurate
5. Know your award and union membership options – keep copies of the award and membership if applicable

Redundancy

The following information has been obtained from the website www.fairwork.gov.au website which is the government department assisting with fair rights for employees.

Redundancy happens when an employer either:

- doesn't need an employee's job to be done by anyone, or
- becomes insolvent or bankrupt.

Redundancy can happen when the business:

- introduces new technology (e.g. the job can be done by a machine)
- slows down due to lower sales or production
- closes down
- relocates interstate or overseas
- restructures or reorganises because a merger or takeover happens

Tax tip: Should you be negotiating a redundancy speak with a tax advisor to ensure you are obtaining the tax advantages available

What's a genuine redundancy?

A genuine redundancy is when:

- the person's job doesn't need to be done by anyone
- the employer followed any consultation requirements in the award, enterprise agreement or other registered agreement.

When an employee's dismissal is a genuine redundancy the employee can't make an unfair dismissal claim.

A dismissal is not a genuine redundancy if the employer:

- still needs the employee's job to be done by someone (e.g. hires someone else to do the job)
- has not followed relevant requirements to consult with the employees about the redundancy under an award or registered agreement or
- could have reasonably, in the circumstances, given the employee another job within the employer's business or an associated entity.
- Helping an employee obtain a tax benefit.

Redundancy Insurance

Redundancy insurance can provide short-term financial assistance if you lose your job. This is not cover for when you choose to leave your job. Some insurers offer it as optional cover on income protection policies.

To be eligible for redundancy insurance, you need to meet the insurer's definition of 'involuntary unemployment' which can mean for example, if you are:

- **An employee** - you have been retrenched from a position of employment that has been paying you a salary, wage or commission.
- **Self-employed** - your business has stopped trading because you haven't been able to meet the business financial commitments.
- **On a fixed term contract** (e.g. 12 months or more) - the contract ceased before a date you previously agreed on, and not by your own choice.

Consulting with employees about major workplace changes

All awards and registered agreements have a consultation process for when there are major changes to the workplace, such as redundancies.

The consultation process sets out the things the employer needs to do when they decide to make changes to the business that are likely to result in redundancies. This must be done as soon as possible after the decision has been made to make these changes.

Consultation requirements include:

- notifying the employees who may be affected by the proposed changes
- providing the employees with information about these changes and their expected effects
- discussing steps taken to avoid and minimise negative effects on the employees
- considering employees ideas or suggestions about the changes

Not all employees are covered under awards; however, there are basic minimum wages and it is advisable to always know your award, Union if applicable and what rights you have in the event you are made redundant.

Termination through Liquidation of a Business

Unfortunately, there are instances where a business runs into insolvency. This is where the business is unable to cover its operating expenses. Even if the assets of the businesses are sold they may not cover the liabilities - including employee entitlements such as annual and long service leave.

When a business is bankrupt, also known as going into liquidation or insolvency, employees can get help through the Governments Fair Entitlements Guarantee (FEG).

The FEG, previously known as the General Employee Entitlements and Redundancy Scheme (GEERS), is available to eligible employees to help them get their unpaid entitlements. This can include:

- wages – up to 13 weeks of unpaid wages (capped at the FEG maximum weekly wage)
- annual leave
- long service leave
- payment in lieu of notice of termination – maximum of 5 weeks
- redundancy pay – up to 4 weeks per full year of service.

It doesn't include:

- superannuation
- reimbursement payments
- one-off or irregular payments
- bonus payments
- non-ongoing or irregular commissions.

Pre-bankruptcy

Before a business goes bankrupt it might go into voluntary administration. Voluntary administration happens when a business can't pay its debts. An administrator is appointed to work out if the business can keep operating or should go into liquidation.

When a business is in voluntary administration the Administrator can provide advice, and help employees seek unpaid entitlements. It is advisable to check your superannuation has all been paid and any annual or long service leave entitlements are considered.

For additional information view www.fairwork.gov.au which is the government department assisting with fair rights for employees.

Do you have the following documentation?	Yes or No	Action to take	By when?
Employment contract			
Timeline of events, performance review records and other correspondence			
Contact details of lawyer, tribunal			
Do you have a financial safety net in the event you are asked to leave work?			
Redundancy Insurance			
Access to other funds to cover everyday living expenses while you seek new employment?			

Key take-away

Dismissal is almost always traumatic, emotionally and financially. Know your rights. Use the information and links here to research your entitlements and develop your Plan B 'just in case'.

Story

When urinating in public isn't cause for dismissal

An employee was employed as a truck driver by a large transport company.

The employee's duties included making long distance and local deliveries.

The employee made a delivery to a large shopping chains Regional Distribution Centre (RDC).

After pressing the RDC's front gate intercom and whilst waiting for the gate to open, the employee was filmed by CCTV to move to the far side of his truck and urinate.

After viewing the CCTV footage, a manager from the RDC complained to the employer about the employee's conduct.

The employer was also advised that the shopping company had banned the employee from all of its sites for 3 months because his actions were in breach of policy.

The HR Investigation

The employer's Group Operations Manager referred the complaint to the employer's HR Manager for investigation.

During the investigation the HR Manager had discussions with the employee about the complaint and informed him of the existence of the CCTV recording.

Following discussions between the Group Operations Manager and the HR Manager, a decision was made to dismiss the employee.

The employee was verbally notified of his dismissal. A subsequent letter to the employee confirmed the dismissal was because of an "act of misconduct."

In consequence, the employee filed an unfair dismissal claim with the Fair Work Commission.

From the court case records: -

In considering whether it is satisfied that a dismissal was harsh, unjust or unreasonable, the FWC must take into account:

(a) whether there was a valid reason for the dismissal related to the person's capacity or conduct (including its effect on the safety and welfare of other employees); and

(b) whether the person was notified of that reason; and

(c) whether the person was given an opportunity to respond to any reason related to the capacity or conduct of the person; and

(d) any unreasonable refusal by the employer to allow the person to have a support person present to assist at any discussions relating to dismissal; and

(e) if the dismissal related to unsatisfactory performance by the person—whether the person had been warned about that unsatisfactory performance before the dismissal; and

(f) the degree to which the size of the employer's enterprise would be likely to impact on the procedures followed in effecting the dismissal; and

(g) the degree to which the absence of dedicated human resource management specialists or expertise in the enterprise would be likely to impact on the procedures followed in effecting the dismissal; and

(h) any other matters that the FWC considers relevant.

A valid reason, but ...

After considering the parties' evidence (much of it conflicting) the FWC accepted that the employee did urinate at the entrance to the RDC and that the conduct was in breach of the employer's Drivers Manual.

The FWC found that a valid reason existed for the employee's dismissal given that his conduct was unprofessional, not acceptable and in breach of the employer's policies.

However, the FWC did not consider any on-going damage occurred to the relationship of the employer.

Further, based on an unrelated prior banning incident, the FWC was not convinced the employee could not have been redeployed during the 3-month ban.

The Verdict

The FWC found the dismissal of the employee was harsh and unreasonable, therefore, he was unfairly dismissed.

The sacked employee sought monetary compensation rather than reinstatement.

At a date to be determined, the FWC will decide as to appropriate monetary compensation, following input from the parties.

The moral of the story is around procedures and their effectiveness. Unfortunately, common sense and the law don't always equate so to avoid potential dismissal Planning Plan B suggest knowing what is expected of you in your work environment.

10 Questions for an Expert

Lawyer Alan Prasad from Nexus Lawyers

1) What kind of insurance is someone able to obtain to protect against losing their job through termination or redundancy?

As I am not an insurance advisor, I am not qualified to advice in this matter. Please consult an insurance broker or an insurance company.

2) I have been dismissed from work and I didn't get any notice who should I contact?

Fair Work Commission. The website is https://www.fwc.gov.au/.

3) What, if any, government support is available?

Fair Work Online (www.fairwork.gov.au) or Fair Work Infoline (13 13 94).

4) My job has been advertised after I was made redundant, is there a recourse I am able to consider as I want to be re-instated in my position?

It could be argued that there was constructive dismissal by your employer. However, one should be conscious that there are time limits to bring claims to Fair Work Commission (within 21 days from the date of termination) or to Courts. Please see

https://www.fairwork.gov.au/how-we-will-help/how-we-help-you/help-resolving-workplace-issues/step-1-find-out-what-we-can-help-with

5) I am under an award and unsure of my union assistance, how do I find this information out?

You would be paying union fees. So, either check your pay slip to find out if you are paying an amount of your wages towards union fees or, ask your human resources.

6) **My employer is spreading rumours about me to the staff who remain, is there anything I can do to stop this?**

   You may have a claim against the employer in defamation. Seek legal advice.

7) **I am unable to get a reference, are they still as important as they previously were?**

   This depends on the industry and your position. For example, references will not be relevant if one was a construction labourer but, would be relevant if in a management position.

8) **The company I worked for has appointed an administrator and I don't think I will be getting paid is there anything I can do to get my unpaid leave and superannuation?**

   Employees who are owed certain employee entitlements after losing their job because their employer went bankrupt or into liquidation may be able to get financial help from the Australian Government. This help is available through the General Employee Entitlements and Redundancy Scheme (GEERS) if their employer went bankrupt or entered liquidation before 5 December 2012, or through the Fair Entitlements Guarantee (FEG) if their employer went bankrupt or entered liquidation on or after 5 December 2012. See http://asic.gov.au/regulatory-resources/insolvency/insolvency-for-employees/

9) **What is an example you have seen where you thought a person had been unfairly dismissed but the FWC tribunal didn't agree?**

   Most unfair dismissal applications before FWC settle and, those that proceed to hearings can be found at https://www.fwc.gov.au/cases-decisions-and-orders.

10) What documentation should I have on file before I come and see a lawyer about a potential action and what is the time frame to do this from when I was sacked?

Unfair dismissal applications should be lodged with Fair Work Commission within 21 days from the date of termination of employment. You must have: (a) copies of employment agreement(s), termination letter recent pay slips, last group certificate, and relevant written correspondences; (b) state the start and end date of employment, details of dates/times (approx.) and facts (ideally, "who said/saw" manner of narration) relied upon to allege unfair dismissal; statement of facts from the employee and/or witness(es) (again, ideally "who said/saw what" manner of narration).

Chapter 8

Disaster occurring while travelling

"I'd rather look back at my life and say, 'I can't believe I did that' than say 'I wish I did that'"

Anonymous

Disaster occurring whilst travelling

A disaster is defined as a sudden accident or a natural catastrophe that causes great damage or loss of life. On the other hand, travelling is for many what life is all about, creating amazing memories that no one can take away.

Unfortunately, disasters can occur at any time to anyone, however, when you are far from home and in a country that does not speak your language, the stress and emotional angst is made that much more horrific. Add additional financial costs and potential risk of medical treatment that is not at the standard you are used to, and it makes sense to plan for a potential disaster whilst travelling.

School holidays even close to home bring an increase in risk of accidents, such as drowning, injuries, bites and car crashes. Tragically, the leading cause of death in Australia among children aged 1-16 is injury with around 150 deaths occurring each year. An injury can happen in the blink of an eye and even when wounds are healed, injured children face issues such as chronic or psychological pain, as well as physical limitations.

And yet very few people think about something bad happening to them and what might happen to their loved ones whilst planning for a holiday? While it is great to be positive, the implications on loved ones if they are required to repatriate you with a medical condition are often financially debilitating.

Many parents have been forced to sell their home to support the medical expenses incurred when a young adult is injured overseas. Unfortunately, the risks taken whilst younger have far great implications if they occur in a foreign country.

How to prepare for travelling disasters?

First Aid Training
Fewer than 1 in 20 Australians have been trained to perform first aid in an emergency. Those who are, are often made to do so by employers so they can comply with Occupational Health and Safety rules. Maybe before going on a holiday find the time to invest in a First Aid course.

Medicinal needs

Consider packing items you may need depending on the travel destination. A first aid kit that includes the basics you may need is a great precautionary measure. Whilst you can often buy similar items, they are often neither of the same pharmaceutical standards nor what your body is used to - so it is wise to be prepared.

A suggested list follows:
- Personal medication
- Band aids
- Insect repellent
- Insect bite relief
- Electrolyte solution or powder
- Pain relief
- Cold and flu tablets
- Sunscreen
- Sun burn cream
- Tweezers
- Nail clippers
- Needle
- Scissors
- Eye drops

Vaccinations

Review the legal requirements and recommended vaccinations for the countries you are going to well in advance. Malaria and other tropical diseases are not something you want to play Russian roulette with. Having seen a young woman in Zimbabwe with malaria and taking someone to hospital in Harare with suspected malaria, I can assure you the implications of not taking precautions are *extremely* unpleasant. Just the use of medical equipment, including needles that may not be adequately sterilised, should be enough to encourage obtaining all the recommended vaccination programs.

Travel insurance

Insurance paid for with your travel agent is often at a premium and a means in which travel agents make most of their commission.

Look at the options you had when making the payment for your trip and then shop online for comparisons for cover and price.

Passport validity

Review your passports at least 6 months prior to travelling to ensure you meet the local country requirements and don't end up needing to pay extra priority payment fees to obtain emergency passports. Also ensure any visas are obtained within the required time frame to avoid stress or the potential for being disallowed into a country.

Register your travel plans

The Australian government has a travel register with www.smartraveller.gov.au and other countries provide similar services to their residents.

By registering in the event of a disaster occurring on a mass scale they can provide consular assistance and communicate with relevant family members updates on events as they happen.

Banks also have programs where you can notify them of your intended travel so that the fraud prevention team do not inadvertently cancel any credit cards whilst you are travelling. Being left without access to funds whilst travelling is a disaster you can easily avoid with a quick update on your online banking.

Advise friends and/or family of your plans

A travel itinerary provided to close family or friends before you leave will help in the event of unexplained loss of contact.

I always prepare a spreadsheet with all travel details and then print out two copies – one to take with me and the other to leave with a close family member.

Evacuation procedures

When going to a place that is at risk of either avalanche, volcanic eruption, earthquake, military attack, fire etc, it is always advisable to be aware of the local evacuation procedures.

Different countries have different warning systems and whilst most people avoid places where this is a real risk, not all travellers do. Having personally been escorted through the Khyber Pass with men armed with AK47s, and through no-go zones in Pakistan, I can attest to the folly of youth and the desire to take risks in the interests of exploration and adventure.

Where you know in advance you are going to take on additional risks, ensure your travel insurance will cover these activities and know that if something unfortunate *does* happen, what the consequences might be.

Prevent disease

Sex, eating and drinking are all normal aspects of our adult lives that carry potential risks that can ruin not only your vacation but may impact on the rest of your life.

Unprotected sex or drinking more than what enables you to make coherent decisions are both bad ideas. Ensure you carry condoms with you in the event there is a likelihood of engaging in a holiday romance.

Food can vary greatly in terms of hygiene in various locations; in particular, third world countries that do not have refrigeration, can result in serious health issues.

Water should only be drunk from the tap where you know it is safe to drink, and if you have a particularly sensitive stomach either boil the water, use a purification bottle, water purification tablets or drink bottled water that has clearly not been previously opened.

Again, even if you are *not* drinking the tap water in the country you are travelling in, be mindful of the ice in your glass. Whilst this is unlikely to cause a severe disaster, I have often seen travellers with a stomach bug that really makes for a bad experience.

Do you have the following documentation?	Yes or No	Action to take	By when?
Travel Insurance			
Travel itinerary and contact details with a family member or friend			
Confirmation of details on Smartraveller			
Copy of passport			
Copy of birth certificate			
Copy of marriage or divorce certificates			
Copy of vaccination record			
First aid certificate			

Key take away

Disasters occurring while travelling are traumatic as they occur in an unfamiliar place with no support network available to assist. If you travel register your travel plans with www.smartraveller.gov.au, take a first aid kit, have the required vaccinations, complete a first aid course and ensure you have travel insurance in place that covers you for ALL your planned activities.

Story

The tragic death whilst travelling of Nicole Fitzsimons

Nicole Fitzsimons would never have hopped on a motorbike without a helmet back home in Australia.

But in the tropical paradise of Koh Samui in Thailand, where it seems like nothing could possibly go wrong, she did. It's what a lot of particularly young tourists do.

The sports journalist who at 24, was in Thailand with her partner, Jamie Keith, to celebrate her first year of working with Channel Nine's The Footy Show when the pair decided to soak up their idyllic surroundings by hiring a motorbike to get around the island.

After a quiet dinner on their final night in Koh Samui, Jamie and Nicole jumped on the bike, without helmets, to drive 1km down the road to where they were staying. As they were pulling into the driveway of the hotel, they were struck by a speeding rider trying to overtake them from the wrong side. Both Nicole and Jamie were knocked off the bike, with Nicole taking the greatest impact.

Back at the Fitzsimons family home in Sydney at 3.37am the phone began to ring.

Kate said, "I'll never forget the sound of that phone vibrating and how my heart immediately stopped because at that hour I knew it wasn't going to be good news."

Kate remembers seeing her photos on Instagram and Facebook during her holiday and in one of her last ever posts, Nicole wrote that 'travelling was so good for the soul'.

And that's what scares Kate the most, because her sister wasn't a risk-seeker — Nicole wasn't over there to go wild and party hard. It was simply that lack of awareness of how dangerous it is on those roads in Thailand and how on holidays we get so relaxed, that before you know it, your safety standards are relaxed as well.

Kate knows her sister never would have never gotten on a motorbike in Australia without a helmet, so she's dedicated to changing the far too carefree attitude we seem to take overseas with us to countries with very different cultural and safety standards to Australia. This mission was born from what she discovered in the weeks after losing her sister – that an Australian tourist dies in Thailand every 2 days. "why are we going over in these places like Thailand, which have the second deadliest roads in the world, and taking such risks? Why is motorbike riding without a helmet promoted as a fun and carefree thing to do?!"

Road accidents are the leading cause of tourist deaths in Thailand and a growing concern for Thai authorities, especially in the holiday hot spots of Koh Samui, Phuket and Pattaya.

Under Thai law, motorcycle riders and passengers must wear helmets but often they are not provided by hire companies or motorcycle taxis, the Department of Foreign Affairs and Trade said.

The United Nations ranks Thailand's roads as the second most deadly in the world, and Australians are 6.5 times more likely to be killed in a traffic accident in Thailand than in Australia.

And figures from DFAT show more Australians die or are hospitalised in Thailand than other country, with 205 deaths and 176 hospitalisations in 2015-16 — both an increase on the previous 12 months.

Nicole Fitzsimons' death, propelled Kate, now 24, to quit her corporate job and dedicate her time to the Nicole Fitzsimons Foundation, which the family set up to educate Australians about travel safety and insurance.

The 2015-16 Consular State of Play, shows of the 10.2 million Aussies who travelled abroad, government assistance was provided to 15,740 people.

The number of people arrested overseas surged 23 per cent to 1551, and imprisonments grew five per cent to 391.

Deaths were also up to 1516 from 1228 the previous year. Most were attributable to sickness or natural causes but 47 related to murders and 214 were the result of accidents.

Of the 315 assaults (up from 234), 136 were of a sexual nature — an increase of 40 per cent on the previous year.

Incidents that triggered the most inquiries or requests for consular assistance were the Bangkok bombing in August 2015, the Paris terror attacks in November last year and the January attack in Jakarta.

Although China had the highest number of Australian prisoners with 61, the US recorded the highest number of arrests with 262 — up from 169.

The most common reason for arrest and imprisonment was drug-related offences followed by fraud and assault.

"The advice to travellers is simple," noted the report. "Don't carry or consume illegal drugs overseas. Ever."

On a brighter note, only eight per cent of Australians travelling overseas did so without insurance but younger people were more likely to tempt fate, with 15 per cent of 18 to 24-year-olds leaving the country with no cover.

"Too many people are willing to travel uninsured," said the report.

"Thirty-one per cent thought it was okay to travel without insurance to a developed country."

An accompanying survey by the insurance industry revealed high proportions of travellers undertaking activities for which they were not insured including skiing, riding an elephant or camel, skydiving and riding a motorbike.

Of all the Aussies who travelled abroad, almost a quarter (24 per cent) experienced an "insurable event" such as flight cancellation or flight delay, medical treatment or lost or stolen belongings.

Kate spends her time now educating these young travellers of the risks involved to prevent other families suffering the same emotional loss of a loved on.

Kate's safety message is particularly aimed at school leavers preparing for Schoolies abroad and overseas adventures that many young Aussies love to take after finishing school. According to travel insurance statistics, of those aged between 17 and 18 who are buying insurance, 90 per cent are heading overseas on their own, predominantly to destinations such as Thailand and Bali.

Kate said without supervision, often travelling for the first time without their parents in destinations where safety standards weren't as high as in Australia, it was essential young travellers knew not to take risks.

"People are so often more focused on finding the best places to eat or where to take the best Instagram photos, and not about how to keep themselves safe and make sure they're coming home with a smile and lots of great memories" Kate said.

"It's the invincible mentality we all have when we're young, so when I open up to them about was like to lose Nicole, they're like, wow — this can really happen."

Kate said she was especially passionate about travel insurance, which Nicole had taken out before her Thailand holiday.

"Straight away, after the call, Mum was stressing to me to find her travel insurance details as they needed to get to Thailand to be by her side. Unfortunately, she did pass away before Mum and Dad made it to her, but the first thing they were met with when they walked through the hospital doors was the hospital bills. They weren't allowed to see Nicole until they were taken care of. I definitely learnt the importance of travel insurance there and then," Kate said.

Kate is an advocate of insurance not just for the financial support, but the moral and emotional care they provide as well.

"Having my parents take off overseas just hours after losing my sister was really scary but I got some peace of mind knowing they were being guided by a company that has great experience in this area. Mum said she barely left the hotel during that time, but her Insurer took care of the bills.

"Initially Nicole was booked on a Thai Airways flight home and Mum asked if a proud Aussie girl could fly home with Qantas instead, and they arranged that. They even sent through red and white roses for her funeral — because Nicole was a mad Dragons fan — and they were with her on her coffin. Their care was phenomenal."

Having shared her story with more than 50,000 students at schools around the country so far, Kate has made a travel safety film with funding from Jetstar and DFAT's Smartraveller.

"It's been a phenomenal journey but what keeps me going is the kids and taking them through the journey of what it's like to lose someone so young and so suddenly and in the last place you'd expect to lose someone," she said.

"You always think your loved one is going to come home safety from a holiday. Those are supposed to be some of the happiest moments of their life, not the moments that are going to end it."

10 Questions for an Expert

Campbell Fuller and Vanessa Billy from Understand Insurance – The Insurance Council of Australia

1) **How do I know what countries are safe to visit?**

   To help Australians avoid difficulties overseas, the Australian Department of Foreign Affairs has created Smartraveller, www.smartraveller.gov.au which contains up-to-date travel advisories for more than 170 destinations as well as a consular information service.

2) **What travel insurance do I need as a single traveller?**

   Travel insurance should be a priority in all travel arrangements, whether you travel regularly, occasionally or you are setting off on a once-in-a-lifetime trip.

   For international journeys, the Australian Government advises that travel insurance is as important as a passport, regardless of your destination.

   The most important thing to keep in mind while purchasing travel insurance is that you need to find a cover that suits your specific individual needs. Not all travel insurance policies cover the same things and you will need to find the cover that is right for you.

   So before purchasing travel insurance, it is worth doing a bit of planning and thinking carefully about your specific circumstances (for example, do you have a pre-existing medical condition?) and the activities you're planning on carrying out while travelling (for example, will you be engaging in activities such as bungee jumping or diving?). The travel insurance market is highly competitive, and consumers have a range of coverage options, so it is worth shopping around to find cover that suits your individual circumstances and travel plans. A very important piece of advice is that price should not be the only criteria you base your decision upon. You might buy a cheap insurance policy, but the policy may exclude activities or circumstances relevant to you.

Read the Policy Document and Product Disclosure Statement (PDS) carefully to make sure that the risks that are important to you are covered – and how much they are covered for.

When choosing a travel insurance policy, you should find out:

- What is included in the policy
- What is excluded, and how this compares with your intended activities
- How to contact your insurer when you are overseas
- What paperwork or information you need to take with you
- The dollar limits for claims on individual items and as a whole
- The proof you might need to make a claim
- The cost of the premium

You should buy a policy that covers you for the full duration of your trip. If you anticipate you may extend your trip, discuss this with your insurer to see if you will be able to extend your policy.

Common limits and exclusions include:

- Pre-existing medical conditions

The PDS will detail the types of pre-existing medical conditions that your insurer won't cover. If you are not sure about whether you have a medical condition that needs to be declared, you should contact your insurer and discuss it. If you have a pre-existing medical condition and you don't tell your insurer about it when you take out insurance, the insurer may refuse to pay some or all of any claim you make later. Many insurers will provide cover for travellers with pre-existing conditions, though they may exclude claims that arise from a specific illness or condition

- Adventure sports

Some activities are excluded from many policies or may require an additional premium to be paid. These may include snowboarding, skiing, surfing, rock climbing, kite surfing, hunting, bungee jumping, parachuting and scuba diving. If you are planning these types of activities, you should look for a policy that covers adventure travel or outdoor activities and make sure your planned pursuits are included in your chosen policy.

Not all policies cover the use of motorised equipment such as motorbikes. Those policies that do will typically only cover policyholders who have an appropriate vehicle licence and are wearing a helmet, and may have restrictions on engine size. Travellers planning to ride motorbikes overseas should read the product disclosure statement (PDS) for the full details of each policy's features, and specifically check that the use of motorbike is included in their cover as well as the conditions under which it is covered. If they are unsure, they should contact their insurer and ask.

- Risky behaviour

Policies will often list exclusions such as loss, injury or damage related to injury under the influence of alcohol or drugs, any self-inflicted injury, the loss or theft of unattended baggage, and the loss or theft of cash

- Disease outbreaks

Many travel insurance policies also have exclusions for claims relating to quarantinable disease outbreaks, such as swine flu

- Civil unrest, war and terrorism

Most insurance policies will not cover claims made in countries where DFAT recommends against travel because of issues relating to terrorism or civil unrest. When preparing your travel plans and before you leave, you should visit Smartraveller to familiarise yourself with advice about the destination to which you intend to travel

- Personal belongings and luggage

Cover may also be limited to a specified amount. Consider additional insurance for expensive items such as jewellery, laptops or camera equipment

- Age

Many travel insurance policies have age limits or restrictions. However, several travel insurers offer policies specially designed for retirees or senior travellers

3) **What is the best kind of policy for a family travelling?**

Most travel insurers offer policies that cover families and couples. When buying travel insurance, make sure all travelling members of your family are listed on your Certificate of Insurance. Most insurers will insure your spouse or de facto partner, your children and your grandchildren. Generally, all children and grandchildren must be dependent and under 25 of age but it's important you check these conditions with your insurer before buying a policy.

As with any kind of travel insurance policy, the best kind of policy will be the one that suits the needs of all members of the family. For example, some people might want to go sailing or diving, so you'll need to check the Product Disclosure Statement to make sure that these activities are included in the policy. You might need to take additional cover for some activities.

4) **If I have travel insurance through a credit card company already do I need to obtain another policy?**

   Some financial institutions provide travel cover as part of their credit card service to their customers. But just because you have insurance through your credit card company doesn't mean that the policy suits you.

   As with any insurance product, it is important to read the Product Disclosure Statement (PDS) carefully to determine how much cover you will receive under this policy and whether there are any requirements you need to meet to qualify for this cover.

   You should also make sure the extent of the cover provided by your financial institution is going to be enough for the place you are visiting and that the activities you're planning to engage in during your holiday are covered by the policy.

5) **If I don't have enough time left on my passport and I only become aware of this at the airport will insurance cover my inability to travel and for an emergency passport?**

   It is your responsibility to make sure, prior to your travel, that you answer all travel documents requirements for your country of destination. Therefore, your travel insurer will not cover any expenses incurred by your failure to obtain the relevant visa, passport or travel documents.

6) **What assistance can I get from the Australian government in the event I need help whilst overseas?**

   Foreign Affairs and Trade (DFAT) website

7) **How do I find the rules for the country I am travelling to, particularly around drinking age, road rules and any other issues that may be important for a traveller to observe?**

   Foreign Affairs and Trade (DFAT) website

The Australian Department of Foreign Affairs' Smartraveller website contains travel advisories and information by country.

8) **My travelling companion has fallen sick and is unable to take the flight home, will the insurance cover my change in flight and additional accommodation to look after them?**

If you and your travelling companion are listed under the same policy, and provided that the illness or injury is disabling, most insurance policies will pay a reasonable additional accommodation and additional transport expenses (at the same fare class and accommodation standards than originally booked) for you and your travelling companion.

Most insurers will require proof of a trained medical practitioner's advice against taking the flight and this advice will need to be accepted by the insurer's emergency team. Make sure you check your insurance Product Disclosure Statement and know the arrangements specific to your insurer prior to departing so you know who to contact should the unexpected happen.

9) **I have a pre-existing medical condition. Can I get travel insurance?**

Yes, you can, but it is very important that you disclose this pre-existing condition prior to taking up travel insurance. If you fail to do this and must make a claim on your travel insurance later, your insurer may reject your claim, leaving you facing potentially massive medical bills overseas.

A lot of existing medical conditions, such as high cholesterol or asthma, will generally be covered by most insurers for free, but make sure you check your Product Disclosure Statement carefully to ensure your condition is covered.

If your condition is not listed in the Product Disclosure Statement, you may still be able to purchase travel insurance for an additional fee. Conditions covered, and additional fees may vary from insurer to insurer so make sure you shop around and find the policy tailored to your needs. The Insurance Council of Australia's free referral tool Find an insurer allows you to search more than 100 general insurance brands through 230 insurance categories to help you make sure you find the insurance policy that suits your specific circumstances.

Some conditions such as heart problems may require further assessment and the insurer will ask you to fill a medical questionnaire before they let you know whether you are able to get cover.

Some conditions however, will not be covered by insurers. This is the case for terminal illnesses or chronic lung disease for example. This does not mean that you will not be able to buy travel insurance. It means that any claim arising from or related to these conditions will not be covered. Other claims (such as loss of luggage for example) may very well be covered. Make sure you talk to your insurer and read your Product Disclosure Statement carefully before taking out a travel insurance policy.

10) Does travel insurance policy cover terrorism?

The Insurance Council of Australia urges travellers to heed advice from Australian authorities relating to terrorist attacks.

Travellers who have been affected by terrorism or whose plans have been disrupted should contact their travel and accommodation providers to seek a refund, credit or alternative travel arrangements.

Travel insurance policies may not cover financial losses resulting from acts of terrorism. However, each policy is different. Some policies may provide cover under certain conditions for affected travellers who have already embarked on their trip. Many policies will cover medical costs. Some will also pay for additional travel and accommodation costs, lost luggage or repatriation, while a small number may cover cancelations due to acts of terrorism.

In other policies, terrorism remains a general exclusion and is not covered at all, so it is important that travellers check each company's product disclosure statement (PDS) if this type of cover is important to them. Travellers who have been affected or are considering cancelling their trip should contact their insurer for guidance.

Helpful guidance is available on the Foreign Affairs and Trade (DFAT) website, (http://dfat.gov.au/) which is frequently updated with the latest travel warnings and advice.

Chapter 9

Dissolution of a business that is unforeseen or due to financial losses

"If you don't drive your business, you will be driven out of business."

BC Forbes

Dissolution of a business that is unforeseen or due to insolvency

We have all heard of the successful entrepreneurs Bill Gates, Warren Buffet, Ray Croc and Richard Branson and, while we might not have the acting talent of Meryl Streep or Leonardo di Caprio, we do all seem to inherently believe if we have a great business idea we will be successful without the need for much business training.

Watching the films "Becoming Warren Buffet" and "The Founder" are great to learn more about the business paths that these men took to create their different but hugely successful empires. Noting they had very different approaches but two underlying themes that drove them: *persistence* and *focus*.

With the lower barriers to entry due to technological advances, more and more people are turning away from traditional employment of 40 hours a week to follow their dream of being in control of their own working life.

However, while starting a business can work for some, it doesn't work for everybody. Passion, a good product, great location, customers and a growing revenue don't always equate to a long term successful business.

Statistically, one in three businesses fail in their first year; two out of four fail by the end of the second year; and three out of four by the fifth year. This doesn't include the statistics where a business continues without one of its founding members.

These are sobering numbers and, based on my professional experience, they can be improved by simply planning for business challenges *before* they arise and remembering that the bottom line matters.

Business Plan

A business plan doesn't need to be overly complicated; there are numerous internet-based companies that will help prepare a business plan (including government organisations). Simply searching for a business plan template and finding one you think works for your business will place you in the three to five per cent of small businesses that prepare a plan when starting from scratch.

Talk to as many people about your idea as possible to uncover objective opinions. Obviously listen with the knowledge you don't have to action them, you just need to hear and listen objectively, taking on board views that are not as emotionally connected to your idea as you are.

Market research at varying levels relevant to your business idea is also prudent. I have seen many businesses start at Bondi Markets go on to achieve International success including Sass and Bide fashion, Uashmama homewares and Samantha Wills jewellery.

There are many more. Market shoppers are often brutally honest and the small capital outlay to determine if your product will find buyers is invaluable and could potentially save you a lot of time and money. My idea of cushions made from retro woollen blankets unfortunately was never going to provide me with the funds for my annual overseas Europe trip. The markets were a great way to test them and get an honest opinion, unlike the positive ones my friends were all providing me with.

Many social media sites also have fantastic communities that comment on start up or growing businesses, and are often used as a sounding board for such business basics as logo, colours, website and product feedback.

Simply searching online for the product or service you are proposing to sell will also give you a good indication of the potential for its success or for new competitors entering your market.

Maintain accurate accounting records

This may sound obvious but, so many new business owners don't understand that once they turn a hobby into a business, legally, they must keep accurate financial records. Various government agencies use the financial information for income tax, payroll tax, workers compensation and financial reporting obligations. Lending institutions will require this information in determining borrowing arrangements. Also, if a business does fail, these records are crucially important as this information will determine financial liabilities.

One business that had to be deregistered after only 2 years was an actors' agency. It had been financed by the owner's father. They had a great business idea but unfortunately the margins on commission as an actors' agent are extremely low and the success needed from the clientele wasn't forthcoming in the time frame required to return a profit. Of course, this two years' of relatively low losses caught the attention of the Australian Taxation Office and they were subject to an audit. Having financial information that was all up-to-date, while some may have considered an unnecessary expense, saved a lot of additional stress that would have occurred had the owner lost the business and then had to recreate the financial information after the closure.

In a lot of ways, having the information, which was based on real time, helped make the decision to close sooner as the numbers clearly showed the loss and not merely money in the bank from family sources.

Maintaining your financial information on real-time, cloud-based accounting software such as Xero (www.xero.com) provides details that, in fact, may make your business salvageable. When a business goes into administration, having accurate records of the financial position can enable a potential buyer to be found, a list of creditors to be easily identifiable and, in the event you are asked to leave a business, information for any disputed amount that may be owing to you.

However, be mindful as to the terms and conditions of all your online subscriptions as to who owns your data. I often liken your files to a car: the owner needs to be the one to sign the car registration papers when transferring ownership; two step authentication (2SA) is like your compulsory third party insurance; a back-up of your files is like being fully, comprehensively insured and, if you only ever drive it in first gear, you are never using the car to its potential. Just as you learnt to drive, you will need to learn how to use the technology that administers your business.

If you are not the owner of your financial data and your accountant, bookkeeper or a staff member is, then what is your plan in the event something (like unexpected death) happens to them, as technically, such information forms part of their estate?

The skill of your accountant/tax agent and bookkeeper also needs to be carefully considered as to whether they have the right attributes to assist your business growth, as well as ensuring the quality of the compliance work, in legal technicalities and lawful minimisation of your tax payments.

In the role I had at Xero I was able to obtain a bird's eye view over more than 250 accounting firms in Northern New South Wales. My experience is, as with lawyers, there are good and bad accountants.

Business questions to ask your Accountant

Below is a list of potential "what if" questions I would ask of a business tax agent/accountant before engaging their services based on the most common entity structures used in Australia. These questions, in my view, cover basic technical awareness of issues for Australian businesses. I'd also recommend you have an accountant who can use the same accounting software you are using. If someone asks you to print a trial balance from an online software program they are wasting your money.

Sole Trader

1. Do I need to register for an ABN and GST? If not now at what point should I do this?
2. If I am about to sign a contract with a distributor for $200,000 what advice would you give me given that amount would be substantially higher than any other income previously?

3. What qualification and how many years of experience do you have?
4. How many other clients in the same type of industry do you have?
5. If there was a potential sale of the business what advice would you give me?
6. I want to go for a research and development grant, can you help me do this?

Partnership

1. Same questions as Sole Trader
2. If we change partners can I keep the same ABN?
3. We don't have a Partnership Agreement – would you be able to prepare this for us?
4. Can we get a different income split from 50:50 each?
5. What asset protection do I have against creditors if my business partner entered into a contract or lease and I didn't sign?
6. I own a rental property with my husband, should we register as a partnership with the ATO?

Company

1. Questions 3-5 from Sole Trader
2. I have been taking money out of the business bank account to pay my mortgage, school fees and other living expenses, what advice do you suggest so I do to not have issues with the Taxation Office?
3. Someone wants to buy my business but not the shares, what does this mean for me personally if I own all the shares?
4. I am doing a lot of research and development on a new software program that we will be selling on a global scale. What issues should I consider?

5. I gave my staff some shares in the company as an incentive to keep my top performers. I am not sure how much they are worth but last year the company made a profit of $500,000 - do I need to do anything?

Trust

1. Questions 3-5 from Sole Trader
2. I want to give my Mum and Dad a taxable income distribution as they have no real income and I have heard from friends this will save me tax. Is this possible?
3. I have children who are 12, 16 and 19. I am paying their school and uni fees; can I give them a trust distribution from the profits of my business?
4. Will you prepare my trust deed, or a lawyer or an online provider? Are there appropriate clauses for income distribution between income and capital, taxable and accounting and for borrowing?
5. I distributed money to a company as the tax rate is (currently) 27.5% versus my top marginal rate of (currently) 49% and lent the money back to the Trust as it is operating the business. Is there anything I need to be careful of?
6. Do I need to do anything before the end of a financial year in relation to who gets the income distribution?

The questions can be read in conjunction with the answers/ issues below. Someone might not know all the answers but I hope they know it's an issue and will either get back to you or refer you to a tax lawyer - this is only my view and I have heard I have high standards but...

Sole trader - issues being registering for GST (note ALL Uber drivers MUST register), capital gains tax issues in transferring a business with a market value to another entity - so $ income levels are important, income splitting of business profits between family members and deciding on when a structure makes sense, their experience and expertise. Tax Institute members are generally highly regarded and Chartered Accountants have what are generally considered the highest entry level exams and university requirements.

Partnership - questions uncover issues around joint and several liability ie if your business partner enters a lease you are liable for it as well, if you change a Partnership it ceases and a new one is formed, new ABNs etc required unless it is a reconstituted continuing entity. Rental properties can generally be held jointly without a need for a partnership tax return - lots of announced changes went through in regards to deductions for depreciation - ask your advisor for current details.

Company - picking up Division 7A issues, capital gains tax exemptions are different if you sell the shares v sell the business from the company, employee share scheme rules are complex and need legal advice and R&D grants are generally a specialist area of advice and dont pay a % - ask for a fixed price.

Trusts – there are a lot of technical issues around the use of Trusts the most basic that I see missed is no minute prepared for the trust distribution at the end of the financial year, Unpaid Present Entitlements, people thinking they can distribute the taxable income but not the actual money to family members and not reviewing the trust deed and ensuring the tax returns and accounts are in accordance with the Deed.

Insurance

A business may go under for more reasons than poor trading performance. Death or ill health of a co-owner, professional negligence, fire or other unfortunate events will each impact the fortunes of a business. Insurance can provide financial cover for your business, including the premises and contents, against loss, damage or theft as well as cover against any resulting financial loss from an insured interruption to the business. The type of cover and amount will depend on the nature of your business and what areas you think are the riskiest. A good business insurance broker will help chose the business cover appropriate for you - but don't forget to ask about their fee structure.

Consider some of the following types of insurance cover available and whether they could help you protect your business: -

- Building & Contents
- Business
- Cyber issues
- Directors Liability
- Glass
- Goods in Transit
- Intellectual Property
- Key Person
- Machinery Breakdown
- Management Liability
- Personal Accident
- Professional Indemnity
- Public Liability
- Tax Audit

Networking with other Business Owners

Having a business network of like-minded people in similar situations helps with issues as they arise in being able to learn from their own personal experiences.

Shared office space – being around other start up

Like the idea of networking, with the increase of cloud-based technology, remote offices are increasing in popularity. These are also creating communities of like-minded businesses in fintech, acctech, and social media, etc. – all of which may support each other. Collaborative businesses learn and scale at a much faster rate than those that typically worked in isolation.

Business Coach

Many business owners have benefited from having a business coach because too often small business owners start without the skills needed to be successful. If this person has a background in accounting, has run a successful business and run training programs, then they should be able to assist you with your business growth.

Compliance rules around income tax, payroll tax, insurance, human resources, workers' compensation, professional indemnity insurance, fringe benefits tax, cashflow management, accounting records, banking, business names, trademarks, contracts, and invoicing etc. - all need to be understood when running a business.

If you have a great creative business idea or product but have always been an employee, then have someone teach you how to run a business. Know what it is you need and what value you are obtaining from your business coach. Are they someone to:

- keep you accountable?
- bounce ideas off?
- train you how to plan for cashflow?
- teach you how to read a profit and loss statement?
- help with a marketing plan?

Knowing your weaknesses and planning to upskill or outsource those areas will increase your chance of business success.

Planning to Fail

If failing to plan is planning to fail does it not also follow that planning to fail leads to failure? In my opinion no it doesn't. There is a huge difference in between preparing for failure and thinking you are going to fail. As they say your thoughts become your reality so thinking you will fail will curtail your growth and success. However, being practical and thoughtful about all the possibilities that may occur even encourages greater success because fears are reduced as time is spent considering the risks involved. And this here is the key word, risk, all large successful organisations plan for failure, they just call it Risk management.

When considering the risk management procedures for your business you will need to consider two areas Disaster Recovery and Business Continuity. Both are necessary and different areas to plan for, before a disaster hits.

Disaster Recovery is the recovery of data and records which are destroyed in the event of a disaster. The most common disaster experienced today is not earthquake, flood, or tornadoes. It's human error or cyber-attack.

Business Continuity is the ability to be back to "business as usual" in the case of a disaster. It is the ability of an organisation to maintain essential functions during, as well as after, a disaster has occurred.

Given the world we live in part of your risk management review should also include a Social Media and Publicity Relations plan as to what happens in the event of a business disaster occurring. If your business relies on the internet to trade then you also need to be ready to handle outages.

Do you have the following documentation?	Yes or No	Action to take	By when?
Business Plan			
Insurance			
Real time accounting records			
Risk management plan			
Original structure documentation ie trust deed, certificate of incorporation			
Business owner agreements			
Passwords for all business applications			
Back up of critical information			
Occupational Health and Safety records			
Any other required government or professional records ie tax agent registration, Certificate of Professional Practice etc			

Key take-away:

Starting a business can be both complicated and exciting. Dissolving a business is usually a mixture of complexity and sadness, especially if it has failed due to an unexpected event or financial failure. Use the links here to support what you need to do and note the 10 questions and answers below for information on business insurance.

8 Questions for an Expert

Insurance Expert Michael Gottlieb owner of BizCover

1. What is Public Liability Insurance and what does it cover businesses for?

Public Liability is the most common type of business insurance, and covers you against the financial risk of being found liable for causing damage, injury or loss to a third party or their property.

The basic idea is that we all have a 'duty of care' to keep clients and members of the public safe and free from harm on our business premises or at another location. If something happens to a client visiting your store, or a member of the public at a seminar you're hosting, you could find yourself in breach of that duty and liable for legal and compensation costs ranging up in the millions of dollars.

Public Liability isn't something you can ignore or self-insure against (unless you have a few million dollars tucked away). Even if you see your business premises as a reasonably safe environment, it only takes a small slip or bump for a client to launch a claim that could financially cripple a small business. We often stress that you don't need to insure against everything, just the things your business couldn't afford to pay for or replace. This is one of them.

2. As a business owner, what kind of Professional Indemnity insurance do I need?

Professional Indemnity insurance (PI) is designed to protect professionals who provide a service, or advice, from the cost of any damages that arise from the delivery of that service or advice. This might be something they've done, some information they've omitted, or it could even be a breach of duty.

The important thing with PI is that it will cover compensation claims and any court costs, even if the claim levelled against you turns out to be invalid. This is crucial.

So, when it comes to Professional Indemnity insurance, the key question is… what service do you provide? If you're a retailer you're more than likely providing a product, so Professional Indemnity insurance probably isn't a priority. However, if you're an accountant, a personal trainer or a consultant, then you'd most definitely want to consider insuring yourself against the damage your service or advice might cause.

3. **I am looking at employing my first staff member, what do I need to do in case of an accident or any issues?**

There are a host of considerations you need to be across when hiring staff for the first time, but the ATO provides a pretty comprehensive guide here: https://www.ato.gov.au/business/your-workers/hiring-workers-for-the-first-time---checklist/

With regards to insurance, employee work-related accidents and illnesses come under Workers' Compensation, which means they're governed by OH&S and WHS laws.

Above and beyond Workers Compensation, and the obvious Public Liability and Professional Indemnity baseline insurances, you may also want to start considering other business insurance options like Management Liability, Employee Dishonesty and Employment Practices Liability.

The thing is, once you start hiring staff your level of risk is instantly amplified across the board. This isn't necessarily a bad thing - it's just something that every business needs to accommodate by asking whether having multiple sets of hands on the business changes the risk of things like theft (by an employee), an alleged wrongful act such as discrimination or harassment, or a statutory breach. You might decide to do nothing. On the other hand, you may go about adding a new policy, selecting an extra option on an existing policy, or increasing the coverage amount you already have.

4. **I've heard a lot of talk about the ATO hiring a bunch of new staff to focus on auditing small & medium size businesses. Is there a way to minimise the damage this could cause to my business?**

   Yes, absolutely. Look, the thought of receiving a call from the ATO is enough to make anyone's palms sweat, even if you have a great accountant and the books are squeaky clean! It's not just stressing about whether you've paid all your taxes either, the whole process of handling an audit can be exhausting and expensive.

   This is where Tax Audit insurance comes in, because it covers all the costs associated with hiring accountants, bookkeepers, financial advisors and extra admin to handle the demands made on you by the ATO. The hope is that you'll save time, money, and an ulcer or two by knowing you have the manpower and the financial recourse to get through what can be a pretty testing period.

5. **What insurance do I legally need to maintain for my business in general?**

   Legally, your main obligation is to organize Workers Compensation insurance as soon as you hire staff. Further to this, you'll need third party personal insurance for any motor vehicles that are used by the business, and some types of companies will be required to carry Public Liability and Professional Indemnity insurance.

   The federal government's website should be the main resource when it comes to mandatory insurance for businesses in each state. There's a handy page here with links to insurance information for each state or territory: https://www.business.gov.au/Info/Run/Insurance-and-workers-compensation/Insurance-in-your-state-or-territory

6. **How do I decide on which insurance will best suit my business needs?**

   Well, you start with the big stuff, the things that could financially sink your business. This will generally mean covering yourself legally with Public Liability and maybe Professional Indemnity. Then you'll want to drill down into other liability insurances like Statutory, Cyber and Management, and assess whether these are primary or particular concerns.

After that, start looking at covering your finances (with personal accident insurance, for example), and your contents and equipment. Again, you don't need take out every form of insurance on the market. You might decide some events are too unlikely to occur, or you may feel like you could handle them on your own. To give you an example, you may not bother insuring your office furniture because replacing your desk and shelving isn't that difficult. However, you may decide that having your data taken hostage as part of a malware attack is something that would do tremendous harm to your business, so you would look at Cyber Liability insurance and how it could protect you from data breaches.

The decision-making process will also be affected by several other variables, such as your budget and your own personal appetite for risk. And you may also be directed by mandatory insurance requirements from government bodies or professional associations.

Ultimately, however, and apart from any legal and compliance obligations, each business owner will be responsible for making their own business decisions, and putting together an insurance plan is part of that decision-making process.

7. **How do you view Income Protection insurance?**

We offer Personal Accident insurance, with injury cover as an option to provide a robust income protection plan. So, if you're unable to work due to accident or illness it will provide up to 85% of your income (up to $3,000 per week) until you're well enough to get back on your feet again.

My view on this is that it's virtually a no-brainer. For most people under 50, your ability to earn an income is your greatest asset, so it makes sense that you would insure against the loss of it. The fact that income protection premiums are generally tax deductible (outside of superannuation) makes it even more attractive.

8. **Cybercrime seems to be in the news a lot lately. How does Cyber Liability insurance work and what does it cover?**

You know, there has been a big shift away from cash transactions and bricks and mortar retailing over the last decade, as the online marketplace has become more prevalent. Where the market goes, criminal activity follows. Not only do businesses have to deal with all the traditional hacking tools such as phishing, DDoS and session hijacking, but cyber criminals are coming up with increasingly sophisticated versions of malware, as we've seen in the recent 'WannaCry' and 'Petya' ransomware attacks.

Unfortunately, small and medium sized businesses are increasingly bearing the brunt of these incursions because they just don't have the resources to guard against them. Criminals are aware these businesses generally can't afford the kind of robust security systems that larger enterprises can muster, so that's who they target. And the consequences can be disastrous. Businesses can lose not only network capability, but critical operational information and, more importantly, sensitive client data.

Cyber Liability insurance won't stop an attack, but what it will do is help cover the business against the associated legal costs and expenses. This might include business interruption, data recovery and investigation, public relations costs, and could even extend to extortion costs and penalties.

There's no magic pill to stopping cybercrime, but a good Cyber Liability insurance plan is a handy recourse if you find yourself a target.

Chapter 10

Depression, Mental Illness or Dementia

"All it takes is a beautiful fake smile to hide an injured soul and they will never notice how broken you really are."

Robin Williams

Depression, mental illness or Dementia

Depression or a mental illness is unfortunately still a taboo subjects in western society. Often seen as a failing or a weakness the mind is one of the last true frontiers for humans to fully discover.

Unfortunately, as a society we are often quick to write off any perceived differences in people who are unlike ourselves. This stigma is starting to change, though, with ex professional athletes and other people with public profiles being more open about their own experiences with depression and mental illness.

Depression

Depression is one of the most common forms of mental illness and is on the increase. Whether this increase is from environmental factors or an increased awareness to seek help is unknown.

While we can all feel sad, moody or low from time to time, some people experience these feelings intensely, for long periods of time and often without any logical reason.

Depression is more than just a low mood – it's a serious condition that affects physical and mental health.

Alarmingly the diagnosis of depression among the young appears to be increasing and is the predominant cause of illness and disability for both boys and girls aged 10 to 19 according to the World Health Organisation.

Mental Illness

There are many different types of mental illness. They can range from mild disorders lasting only a few weeks through to severe illnesses that can be life-long and cause serious disability.

Mental illnesses can affect people's thoughts, mood, behaviour or the way they perceive the world around them. A mental illness causes distress and affects the person's ability to function at work, in relationships or in everyday tasks.

Unfortunately, due to the stigma and discrimination that exists about 10% of people with mental illness eventually die by suicide, as compared with one to three per cent of the general population.

Although mental illness is treatable, about two thirds of people with mental illnesses do not seek any treatment. Psychological therapy, medication and lifestyle changes can be effective for mental illness and we recommend you seek the advice of a medical professional.

Dementia

Dementia describes a collection of symptoms that are caused by disorders affecting the brain. It is not one specific disease.

Dementia affects thinking, behaviour and the ability to perform everyday tasks. Brain function is affected enough to interfere with the person's normal social or working life.

The most common types of dementia are Alzheimer's and Parkinson's disease.

Whilst it normally impacts people over the age of 65 there are instance where it impacts people at a much younger age, Michael J. Fox being the most notable celebrity to be impacted from a diagnosis at the age of 29. Whilst battling the condition for 25 years he has also formed a foundation to research a cure for this disease www.michaeljfox.org/

Planning for Depression, Mental Illness or Dementia

I personally experienced the diagnosis of my father at 55 with bipolar disorder, which is a chronic mental health condition exhibiting strong changes in mood and energy. People experiencing bipolar disorder can have depressive episodes which include low moods, lethargy, and feelings of hopelessness or hypomanic episodes. My father experienced hypomanic episodes and so watching an extremely intelligent man suddenly go from "normal" to "crazy" was an extremely traumatic experience for all family members. Thankfully, with appropriate medication and treatment this was able to be managed. This experience did teach me not to judge people with mental health issues as being weak. It is as much an illness as a physical injury and not able to be controlled no matter how strong or intelligent a person is.

Whether it be depression or a mental health illness the planning you can put in place is really around your ability to earn an income, cover potential medical expenses and providing authority for someone to make decisions on your behalf if required.

Available Insurance Options

It is hard to cope with stressful situations when you are depressed and then financially impacted by an inability to earn an income. Below are three insurance options you can consider which are also covered in Chapter Seven: -

1. **Income Protection**

Income protection insurance replaces the income lost through your inability to work due to injury or sickness. It is an important consideration for anyone who relies on an income. It is especially suitable for self-employed people, small business owners or professionals whose business relies heavily on their ability to work.

2. **Total and Permanent Disability Insurance**

Total and permanent disability (TPD) insurance provides cover if you are totally and permanently disabled. Your insurer will define TPD as either when you:

- You can't work again in **any** occupation, or
- You can't work in your **usual** occupation

TPD insurance helps cover the costs of rehabilitation, debt repayments and the future cost of living.

Each insurer has different definitions of what is and isn't considered to be totally and permanently disabled. Being off work for a year is NOT 'permanently disabled'. Ask lots of questions so you know exactly what you're getting.

An insurance broker who can run through your questions and personal circumstances will help obtain cover that is both reasonable and meets your needs.

3. Trauma Insurance

Trauma insurance provides a one-off lump sum in the event you are diagnosed with a specified illness or injury. These policies include the major illnesses or injuries that will make a significant impact on a person's life, such as cancer or a stroke. It's a great financial back-up plan that can be used to cover medical treatment, time off work and modifications to your home for physical accessibility.

Assign Decision Making Authority

Some of the topics covered in the preparation of an Estate Plan are also relevant to not being able to look after your own day to day needs.

Power of Attorney

An Enduring Power of Attorney is a legal document where you appoint a person of your choice to manage your assets and financial affairs if you are unable to do so due to illness, an accident or your absence.

A medical power of attorney allows you to appoint someone to make decisions about your medical treatment if you become mentally or physically incapable of deciding for yourself.

A friend recently explained the process she had to go through to have her elderly father declared incapable of making his own decisions; she sought to be granted the right to make decisions regarding placement in a nursing home, sale of his home and investment decisions.

Being made to go through all the reasons of either incapacity or incompetence in front of a loved one, as well as in front of strangers, to prove they no longer have the capacity to make their own decisions was a horrific and traumatic experience both for her and her father.

To be able to make an enduring power of attorney the adult must have 'full legal capacity'. This means the person must know and understand:

- the nature and extent of their own estate (land, property and financial assets)
- that an enduring power of attorney will give the attorney complete authority to deal with all aspects of their property and financial affairs (provided that such dealings are in the interests of the person making the enduring power of attorney).

Adults with impaired decision-making abilities, such as those with a psychiatric condition, dementia, an intellectual disability or an acquired brain injury may not be able to execute an enduring power of attorney.

Please, if you don't do anything else after reading Planning Plan B at least get a Will and an Enduring Power of Attorney in place.

Each State in Australia has information on the process you would need to go through in the event a loved one doesn't have this document legally documented.

http://www.publicadvocate.wa.gov.au/E/enduring_power_of_attorney_frequently_asked_questions.aspx?uid=7345-1823-2997-6522

Warning: It is important to note that the power of attorney (PoA) provides that person with the legal authority to act on your behalf and in your best interests, they cannot use the money for their own benefit. Should you suspect someone is misusing a PoA, and the person they are acting for is suffering from impaired mental capacity, you could consider making a complaint to the Office of the Public Guardian. This is particularly important for aged care workers as the potential discovery of missing funds when the estate is distributed has the potential for legal dispute amongst the beneficiaries.

Advanced Care Plan

These documents together provide an **Advanced care plan** that should ensure your care is to the standard you would have set should you have been able to make those decisions yourself.

The advance care planning process encourages you to reflect on what is important to you, your beliefs, values, goals and preferences in life. It explains how you want to be cared for if you reach a point where you cannot communicate decisions about your medical care. It keeps you involved in your medical decisions, both now and in the future, whether you are healthy or have an illness.

Each State in Australia has a Government Department that provides information as to what you need to consider. The information below is from the NSW website https://www.myagedcare.gov.au/end-life-care/advance-care-planning

In summary, an advance care plan may include:

- an Advance Health or Care document outlining your preferred wishes
- an enduring power of attorney (or another similar document)
- a letter to the person who will be responsible for your decision making
- an entry in your medical record on www.myhealthrecord.gov.au

Increase in claims from depression and anxiety

Recent insurance company data show claims for income protection — where most depression and anxiety claims surface —are as high as claims from accidents and injury, and are twice as high as cancer pay-outs. The increase in mental health pay-outs have, in fact, been so high that insurance premiums across the board are increasing.

Whilst the exact causes of depression remain unclear, it is often linked to periods of chronic or excessive stress. Stress related factors often being those discussed in this *Planning Plan B* being divorce, death of a loved one, a serious accident, illness or disability. Another physical side effect of a stressful event occurring is stress hives.

Stress Hives

Hives often develop when you have too much stress, tension or anxiety in your life. When you expose your body to excessive stress, whether it be over a short period of time or a long period of time, your body's immune system starts to not function effectively.

When your immune system is out of kilter it starts sending histamine into the body to fight off what is ailing you - stress. Your body forms an allergic reaction to stress. Unfortunately, stress cannot be entirely eliminated with histamine, so instead, the histamine just causes hives to appear on your face, neck, chest and other parts of your body.

Whilst creams can treat the symptom, they don't help the actual cause of the problem. Learning to know your body, and how you can relax, will play a huge part in reducing this short-term stress to not cause long term damage to your health.

Warm baths, yoga, walking the dog, watering the garden, knitting, attending a retreat, meditation, kicking a ball - whatever reduces stress, is the most important time to make these activities a priority.

Two women who helped me with my stress management were Dr Karen Coates http://www.drkaren.com.au/ and Saimaa Miller http://www.saimaamiller.com/

and I highly recommend reading the books they have written to optimise your health.

With the events that occurred to me, I did suffer from stress hives and whilst medically some may argue this isn't linked, my experience proved to me it definitely is. Add hives to the mental and practical issues when you are dealing with traumatic events and it can act as the "straw that breaks the camel's back" and result in the inability to function normally. The unattractiveness of itching and scratching is not something you want to add to events such as post-divorce, dissolution of business, sale of home, starting a new business, single parenting and venturing out into the dating scene after 13 years. I had blisters appearing all over my body and the discomfort and irritation was all consuming for several weeks. They only disappeared whilst I was able to relax on a holiday.

Meditation and Mindfulness

A lot of research is being undertaken on understanding how the mind works and, whilst outside the scope of this book, it is worth mentioning that in times of high stress meditation is an option to consider reducing the impact on your health.

Regardless of the scientific evidence, sitting and focusing on breathing slowly can significantly change the impact stress has on your body. *"... diaphragmatic breathing is considered by many to be the simplest and most effective form of controlled respiration in the reduction of excessive stress."* Dr George S. Everly M.D.

Taking care of your health, particularly with the increased knowledge of our gut health making huge inroads into treating mental illnesses, is a preventative measure that may reduce the likelihood of depression or mental illness.

Increasing stress levels, toxins, and electronic magnetic fields are being researched to find a correlation to the increase in both physical and mental health issues occurring in the Western World. Though this is outside my area of expertise, the premise of a "checklist" style of preparing a Plan B and really optimising your personal health should be all part of your daily Plan A.

Based on my own experience of extremely high stress levels, the benefits of yoga, massages, healthy eating and warm baths helped prevent me from sliding into a deeper depression.

Do you have the following documentation?	Yes or No	Action to take	By when?
Income protection insurance			
Total and Permanent Disability Insurance			
Trauma Insurance			
Power of Attorney			
Enduring Power of Attorney			
Advance care plan			
Password information for online applications with a close family member or friend			
Private Health Insurance			

Key take-away:

We all suffer melancholic 'downers' now and then but these are as nothing compared to conditions such as clinical depression, mental illness and dementia, articles on all of which appear regularly in both the professional and public media. As society has become more enlightened on these topics, so help has been more widely available. The links above together, with Philipa Thornton's insightful article below, are here to provide you with a resource to explore further, which we encourage you to do as part of your Plan B.

Wisdom from an Expert Philipa Thornton Executive Director of the Resource Therapy Institute of Australia

We are emotional beings and it is natural and normal to feel sad and disappointed when life doesn't go according to our plan. As a mentor of mine Gordon Emmerson says, "Beginnings and endings are fragile things." (Emmerson, 2014).

Whether you experience the death of a loved one, diagnosis with chronic illness, pain or disability, personal or professional rejection, the ending of a significant relationship, property losses, financial crisis, you are likely to feel many emotions.

Formerly, it was thought bereavement around losses, if done 'correctly', fit into discrete stages and include shock, disbelief, anger, guilt, bargaining and depression. Current research tells us the time it lasts and how we feel and respond to grief varies from individual to individual. There is no right or wrong way or proper length of time, or sequence of emotions to be experienced, for dealing with personal loss or negative major life events.

It is appropriate to you give yourself time to mourn, incorporate and understand the situation and its impacts. Some people cry a great deal, others not at all. This is completely normal. There is not set course for 'correct' mourning. Be gentle with yourself, especially if the loss is someone whom you were very close to.

An intense level of confusion can surround a person in an unwanted or unexpected tragic loss, as in the case of suicide, an accidental death, homicide, or relationship breakdown. This deep confusion can cause sleeplessness, guilt, shame, prolonged grief and rumination (the inability to let a thought go, often this takes the form of "why did this happen?" "Why did she leave me?"). A person will usually be able to continue to get on with most areas of life with little interference at work and have energy to keep up most things day to day.

If a person is so upset that life has not turned out how it was planned, for example, because of being retrenched or a marital separation, this upset can block a person from fully participating in life in a positive manner (Emmerson, 2014). Shutting out enjoyment of a relationship (as in the case of infidelity) or life itself.

Take the person who is retrenched from what they thought was their lifetime job after many years of being with an employer. This disappointment may stop a person from engaging with life, leading to depression, despair and suicidal thinking or action.

It is a person's interpretation of the disappointment that is of importance here, not what happened. Two people can experience the same event and one can become depressed while the other may not be significantly bothered. For instance, the loss of a pet may be a fact of life and a sad loss for one, while for another, this can be a devastating loss.

If you are feeling stuck in overwhelming disappointment, confusion, and expectations, then blame and resentment around this this will block you from moving forward in your life. You may need therapy to help you process and let go of unresolved emotions and fast track your healing.

People often use the term depression in day-to-day conversations when they are describing a level of distress or unhappiness after an unpleasant event that has happened to them. This is really a short-term low mood or down time we all go through in life.

Depressive illness is more than this occasional down mood. It is when your mood state is severe, lasts for longer than a few days and interferes with your ability to function in your home life or at work. Warning signs you may be slipping into depression include:

- Loss of self esteem
- Loss of libido
- Lowered concentration, poor memory or ability to think clearly

- Change in appetite or weight (loss or gain)
- Decreased motivation, a sense of hopelessness, not worth the effort and things are meaningless
- Sleep pattern changes – insomnia, broken sleep or excessive sleeping.
- Low energy levels or chronic tiredness
- Anxiety and restlessness
- Physical slowness or a sense of being weighed down
- An intense and persistent sadness, low mood, blame, pessimism, anger, irritability, or guilt
- An inability to enjoy previously positive experiences, (anhedonia), and a sense of hopelessness that continues for weeks or months.
- Recurrent thoughts of death or suicide

These signs are often in evidence for more than two weeks and not due to a medical condition. A mourning period can take a considerable time, even several years.

If you are experiencing the above symptoms not budging for a few months, it is a good idea to seek out a mental health professional.

Psychological Treatment

Psychological therapy is the first line treatment for depression. Depressive illness is a physical illness and is definitely fast tracked with good therapy. It has the added benefit of building your resilience in the future, offering you an opportunity to learn and grow.

We are privileged in Australia to have the **Better Access Initiative to Psychiatrists, Psychologists and General Practitioners through the Medicare Benefits Scheme**, a Government program. This is available to people with a diagnosed mental disorder - depression. You can access Medicare rebates for up to ten individual and ten group sessions per calendar year. Medicare rebates are not available for couple sessions, but you may be eligible for your solo sessions.

Your doctor will make an assessment and prepare a GP Mental Health Treatment Plan. You can state your preferred Australian Health Practitioner Regulation Agency therapist or ask your GP for a referral to psychologists or other allied mental health practitioners for these sessions through the Medicare Benefits Scheme (MBS). Private health insurance can also have psychology session rebates; this depends on your insurance provider's package and your insurance coverage; check with your insurer.

To a receive the Australian Government's Better Access initiative from the MBS, you will need to be given a diagnosis of a mental disorder from a medical practitioner as specified by the Diagnostic and Statistical Manual of the American Psychiatric Association fifth edition (DSM 5). However, many people's issues will not necessarily fit into the DSM 5 criteria for a mental disorder.

> There may be implications of a diagnosis of a mental disorder for your future employment. Mental health diagnoses are subject to the same privacy requirements as physical health diagnoses, so there is no hard and fast rule. However, if an employer made disclosure of a health (physical or mental) issue, on valid, work related safety/capability grounds, a requirement for application for the position, it would be at an applicant's own risk, not to comply with this requirement. Similarly, if while in a position, an individual was affected by a mental health issue, such that it compromised their ability to meet job requirements, it would seem sensible to inform the employer of this fact. Indeed, you may get more support and assistance from your employer.

While your medical records are confidential. Some insurance companies, employers and professional bodies require you to declare a mental illness diagnosis. I counselled a woman* escaping from domestic violence that was referred by Victims Services (This is a free counselling service and support for victims of crime http://www.victimsservices.justice.nsw.gov.au/). She applied to join the Police Force and honestly declared that she was in therapy. Initially they refused her application on these grounds. As her mental health treatment provider, I wrote a letter to inform and recommend her as a person of good standing, honest, of solid character, with the ability to seek assistance to resolve issues (Post traumatic Stress Disorder, PTSD), all excellent qualities for a Police recruit. This lady was then accepted into the Police. *(*Actual details changed to protect client confidentiality.)*

It is a sign of good mental health when you seek appropriate help, use reflection and learning about yourself and your responses, as it can assist you to perform better in all areas of your life.

Antidepressants

Antidepressant medications do have their place in the treatment of severe and chronic depression but probably not for mild to moderate cases.

An antidepressant's main aim is to relieve the symptoms of depression and as such will not resolve the cause. People with more severe forms of depression – bipolar disorder and psychosis, may need to be treated with a variety of medications. These may include mood stabilisers, anti-psychotic drugs and antidepressants.

Unfortunately, many antidepressants have unpleasant and potentially harmful side effects, so do your research. These can include weight gain, sexual dysfunction, sedation, emotional flatness, or an increase in suicidal thoughts. Please monitor and consult with your doctor about the potential side effects and report any disturbing ones to them.

Antidepressants are not physically addictive. However, it is important to remember that when you stop taking the medication, you do so gradually, to prevent the unpleasant symptoms of sudden withdrawal, for more information visit https://www.nps.org.au/australian-prescriber/articles/stopping-antidepressants This must be discussed with your doctor.

The rise of antidepressant use could be linked to the out-dated idea that depression was the result of a chemical imbalance (France, 2007). It was once thought neurotransmitters and serotonin was depleted. Scientific research has subsequently demonstrated the erroneous nature of the chemical imbalance hypothesis, in the causation and maintaining of depression.

According to an article in the Scientific American, (Arkowitz & Lilienfed, 2014), pharmaceutical company marketing, in part fostered the erroneous belief depression was a biological illness. The drug manufacturers used to foster the chemical imbalance hypothesis, as many of the medications they manufactured, do increase serotonin, and other neurotransmitters. Indeed, many antidepressants are known as selective serotonin reuptake inhibitors (SSRIs), which leave more serotonin available in the brain. However just because a drug reduces symptoms of a disease, it does not follow that those symptoms were caused by a lack of those chemicals the drug promotes. That would be like saying, as aspirin relieves headaches, headaches are caused by a deficiency of aspirin and this is certainly not the case. (Arkowitz, et.al, 2014.)

Depression, and its psychiatric cousins –Bipolar Disorder and Psychosis

It's wonderful news we are not merely at the mercy of our brain chemicals. Current research tells us depression is 10 times more common in people born since 1945, as compared to those born pre-1945 (Seligman, 1988). This means essentially ten times as many people are becoming depressed compared to fifty years ago. Yes, slightly alarming but it is also helpful to know. Our genes cannot change this quickly, which leads scientists to the idea that major depression and its exponential increase are associated with changes in our society and lifestyles.

Depression is not an inevitable consequence of adverse life events, our genes or our biology. Only a small minority of people exposed to difficult situations go on to develop major depression. Phew!

Depression is a member of a group of psychological conditions known as mood disorders. Mood disorders includes dysthymia, (chronic low mood), bipolar disorder, which used to be known as manic depression and depressive psychosis.

Bipolar disorder symptoms include very severe mood swings. These extreme emotional states range from intense elation, (mania), to extreme, non-ambulant, depression. Someone in a bipolar episode will have periods of time where they experience great energy and exhilaration for days, weeks or months. At other times, they will experience very deep depression. These highs and lows are severe and are far greater than most people will experience in their lives. People experiencing severe episodes will be unable to deal with everyday life. This illness often begins in the late teens or twenties but rarely after 40 years of age.

Symptoms of mania include:

- feeling euphoric: very exhilarated or elated
- feeling restless, inability to sit still
- aggressive behaviour,
- becoming extremely irritable, and agitated
- talking very quickly, rapid speech
- engaging in risky activities,
- sexual drive elevated, unsafe sexual encounters
- thoughts racing quickly through your head,
- poor concentration,
- loads of energy,

- spending too much money on the wrong things,
- reduced need for sleep, staying up for days
- feeling self-important, grandiosity
- impaired judgement, inability to make reasoned decisions
- and misusing drugs or alcohol.

Bipolar disorder is what is known as a cyclical illness, as people tend to cycle in and out of manic and depressive phases. At the extreme, bipolar people can experience delusions and hallucinations.

As with many mental health conditions, the cause of bipolar is not fully known. It is likely to be a mix of genetic and environmental factors, like stress or childhood abuse.

Treatment usually involves psychotherapy and targeted medications. These medications are called mood stabilisers, lithium being one example; people are often prescribed a combination that can include antidepressants and anticonvulsants. This is a lifetime condition, which requires medical care to help prevent relapse. In severe cases people have recklessly endangered their physical and financial well-being. A person experiencing a manic episode may be involuntarily hospitalised for their safety, by a medical professional.

Psychosis is a clinical term that describes a group of mental illnesses mainly characterised by a loss of contact with reality in the form of delusions, hallucinations and extreme irrational thinking (thought disorder). The first line treatment for psychosis is pharmacotherapy – antipsychotic medications.

There are medical conditions that can cause psychosis, depression and anxiety. Therefore, physical conditions must be ruled out. I have suffered depression myself, brought on by hypothyroidism, because of a viral illness: Hashimoto's Thyroiditis. I need to take a thyroid boosting medication daily otherwise I will become unwell.

Here are some of the physical illnesses that can have a psychiatric presentation: brain tumour, hypoglycaemia (low blood sugar), Diabetic Ketosis, HIV, Mononucleosis, Delirium, Viral illnesses, Liver diseases, Alzheimer's, Wernickes-Korsakoff's syndrome: acute thiamine (vitamin B6) deficiency, Delirium Tremens from alcohol withdrawal.

While it is highly unlikely that a psychological disturbance is caused by a physical illness (less than 10%) it is worth getting a physical check-up from your health professional before seeking psychological help. (Diamond, 2002) https://www.alternativementalhealth.com/psychiatric-presentations-of-medical-illness-2/

REFERENCES

Arkowitz, H. Lilienfed, S, (2014) *Is Depression just bad chemistry?* Accessed on 28 September 2017 https://www.scientificamerican.com/article/is-depression-just-bad-chemistry/

Craft, L, L., Pena, F. M. (2004). *The benefits of exercise for the clinically depressed.* Journal of Clinical Psychiatry.2004; 6(3): 104–111.

Cruwys, T, Haslam, S,A., Dingle, G.A., Jetten, J. Hornsey, M. J., Chong. E.E.D., Oei.,T.P.S.(2014). *Feeling connected again: Interventions that increase social identification reduce depression symptoms in community and clinical settings.* Journal of Affective Disorders. April 20, 2014. Volume 159, Pp. 139–146. Accessed 1 October 2017. http://www.jad-journal.com/article/S0165-0327(14)00057-3/fulltext

Diamond, 2002 accessed 1 October 2017 https://www.alternativementalhealth.com/psychiatric-presentations-of-medical-illness-2/

Emmerson, G. J. (2014*). Resource Therapy The Complete Guide with Case Examples & Transcripts.* Blackwood Victoria, Australia: Old Golden Point Press.

France, C. M., The *"Chemical Imbalance" Explanation for Depression: Origins, Lay Endorsement, and Clinical Implications.* In *Professional Psychology: Research and Practice*, Vol. 38, No. 4, pages 411–420; August 2007.

Sánchez-Villegas, A., Henriquez_Sánchez, P. , Ruiz-Canela, M. Lahortiga, F. Molero, P. Toledo, E. And Martinez-Gonnzález. M. A., 2015. *A longitudinal analysis of diet quality scores and the risk of incident depression in the SUN Project.* BMC Medicine 2015 13:197.

https://bmcmedicine.biomedcentral.com/articles/10.1186/s12916-015-0428-y

Seligman, M. E. P. In J. Buie (1988) *'Me' decades generate depression: individualism erodes commitment to others.* APA Monitor, 19, 18. "People born after 1945 were ten times more likely to suffer from depression than people born 50 years earlier."

Chapter 11

Distressed sale of a home

"Home is where the heart is"

Anonymous

Distressed Sale of Home

The loss of a much-loved family home with potentially years of family memories can be one of the most stressful events in life.

Boys and girls all likely grow up with different dreams around a family home, however when you have achieved this goal and are proud of your achievements the unexpected loss of your home can be devastating.

A home can be lost though fire, flood, earthquake, divorce or financial change in circumstances.

Dream Home

My dream was realised when my home was featured in House and Garden in 2012 after a nine-month renovation with the quote being "my forever home". Within a few years I lost my husband, business, beautiful home and had to rehome the family dog (luckily to an awesome family the Hartigans). Had the business change not been so close to the relationship split, I would have bought my ex out or held on for 2 years before having to sell the home to give the children one less change. However, the reality of the situation was that "my forever home" had to be sold.

Being forced to sell a home and re adjust living circumstances has all sorts of implications. It impacts on status, comfort, flexibility, social events and the ability to have a live-in au pair, who may be required to help with work and child raising. Whilst I appreciate I was fortunate to have a home to sell, when you have made sacrifices and worked hard to achieve this, it is hard emotionally to need to sell a home as part of a relationship breakdown.

Everyone's financial circumstances are different but the stress of buying and selling a home already comes into the Holmes and Rahe stress scale at 25 points. Adding in the stress of it not being a planned move, I am sure it would sit more around 75 points.

Some of the reasons for a distressed sale have already been discussed in this book and, if appropriately planned for, hopefully result in not needing to sell your family home. They include but are not limited to: -

1. **Death**

    A death in the family can lead to a distressed property.

    - *Joint Ownership*

        If the home is owned by two individuals and one passes away, the remaining person may not be able to fulfil the mortgage commitment on their own. They may put the property up for sale at a discounted price in the hope of getting it sold quickly before they default on their mortgage.

    - *Sole Ownership*

        If a property has a single owner and he or she passes away, the property is usually put up for sale in something known as an estate sale. Again, the intent here is not always to get the highest price possible, but often to unload the property quickly and divide the money up among the beneficiaries.

    - *Public Trustee Sale*

        State governments have departments that aim to look after the estates of people who don't have someone else to arrange it for them, or who haven't set up a valid Estate Plan. In New South Wales this department is called NSW Trustee and Guardian, and part of their role in the financial management of an estate is to liquidate assets, i.e. sell property to obtain cash for distribution. When a Public Trustee is selling a home, it is for immediate sale so may not be at the best timing to maximise the sale proceeds.

2. **Divorce** – with and without kids

    If a couple who own a property together separate, the home is often put up for sale. Since both parties need to sell the property for emotional and/or financial reasons, these types of properties are often priced to sell quickly rather than to get top dollar for the property.

3. **Job Relocation**

   Property owners who must move unexpectedly due to a job relocation might be motivated to sell their current residence quickly if they want to buy in the area they are relocating to. This often leads to a willingness to accept a lower offer than they would have otherwise entertained to avoid two mortgages or bridging finance.

4. **Financial**

   A distressed property often arises due to some sort of financial strain. Whether a job loss, pay cut, divorce, medical condition, or some other financial drain, the owner is no longer able to pay the mortgage, rates or services on the property. The owner may be keen to sell before they miss a mortgage payment, so they are willing to accept a discounted price for their property to avoid doing so.

5. **Property Condition**

   The condition of the property, unfortunately, may also result in a reduced sale price. Some common property conditions that can lead to reduced sale prices are:

   Properties That Need Updating- Properties that are in poor condition will not generally obtain the highest price, so buyers who are willing to take on these renovations can often purchase the property at a reduced price.

   Properties That Need Extensive Renovation– Some properties need layout changes, additional space, plumbing and electrical work, a new roof, changes to the foundation or even a full renovation. These properties that need more than a few simple updates are often steeply discounted because the demand from buyers is that much smaller.

Property Renovations in Mid-Construction- These are properties with renovations that were started, but not finished. For example, a developer buys a property, starts renovating, but runs out of money and is unable to complete the renovation. The developer then puts the property up for sale to attempt to recover some money from it or cut their losses. In these properties, work often needs to be completed before the property is certified as occupiable.

6. **Partnership Dispute**

A distressed property can be the result of a dispute or falling out between two parties who own a property in a joint venture agreement. They may have to unexpectedly sell the property once their relationship breaks down, so an interested buyer can benefit from their need to sell.

7. **Bank Foreclosure**

Properties that have been foreclosed on, and are now owned by the bank, can often be sold at a lower price than market value. The lender's goal is simply to unload the property to extinguish the outstanding debt. Foreclosure can occur when the borrower fails to make repayments for more than three months in a row. The lender can move to evict the borrower and put the home up for sale. Such sales can be distressing and soul-destroying for the current occupant. There are unfortunately enough homes that are foreclosed that there is a business specialising in forced home sales. http://www.forcedsale.com.au/properties

How can you protect your family from a distressed sale of your home?

Unfortunately, life can throw you curve balls and all the planning in the world might not be able to prevent you from needing to sell your home in times of stress. Below are some ideas on how to best prevent this occurring. I would also recommend reading books on investment including The Barefoot Investor by Scott Pape or Rich Dad Poor Dad by Robert Kiyosaki as you greatly reduce the risk of financial distress if you are not over extended with debt.

Lenders Mortgage Insurance (LMI)

Many years ago, when a bank provided finance, mortgage insurance was compulsory. That was because Lender's Mortgage Insurance (LMI) is an insurance policy that protects the lender from financial loss if the borrower can't afford to keep up the home loan repayments. Having said that, in the event a loan is defaulted on, and the home needs to be sold, in Australia, any shortfall is still required to be paid back to the bank. This insurance in the current market may reduce the risk of potential bankruptcy so speak with a licensed adviser to determine what is best for your personal circumstances.

Under the terms that are included in most LMI policies, a financial institution can make a claim if the borrower defaults on the loan, and the sale of the property doesn't equal the value of the mortgage

Lenders' mortgage insurance is added directly to your home loan, so it's not technically an upfront fee – but you still pay for it.

Generally, the size of your deposit will impact on the requirement for LMI and also your employment history. Self-employed people, who will increase in numbers in the age of the Digital Revolution, will find it harder to prove they meet the traditional banks' requirements to service the loan repayments.

Mortgage Protection Insurance

Mortgage protection insurance is a simplified form of personal insurance available to those with a mortgage, to cover the cost of your regular monthly mortgage repayments if you die, became seriously ill with a medical condition, or even lose your job.

If you believe this type of planning is suitable, it is advisable to speak with an insurance broker to discuss your personal circumstances.

Income Protection Insurance

Income protection insurance can provide you with a monthly benefit if you are unable to work for a certain period because of illness or injury. This insures you for a set level of your income (commonly 75% of your gross salary) and will pay you at that level until you are able to return to work or for the agreed benefit period – whichever is sooner. Different premium levels will also be impacted by waiting periods prior to the payments being made by the insurer and the excess amounts.

If you believe this type of planning is suitable it is advisable to speak with an insurance broker to discuss your personal circumstances.

Conservative Mortgage and Finance

Every property purchaser has a different investment risk profile and it is worthwhile understanding your own profile. There are a lot of tests on the internet, and a financial planner can also help provide this information. My experience as an accountant is that people with the same income and opportunities can save or spend based on this inherent characteristic, so it is important to understand how your attitude to money impacts you and your family.

If you have a higher risk profile you might be comfortable with a high mortgage however in the event something negatively happens, you won't have the same financial buffer a less conservative investor/home owner will have.

If you are new home owner and unsure about what are the relevant amounts of your income to be using for a mortgage repayment

Early access to Superannuation Funds

There are very limited circumstances to access your super savings early. These circumstances relate mainly to specific medical conditions or severe financial hardship.

The Australian Taxation Office provides information on the circumstances for partial or full release of your super before you reach preservation age.

https://www.ato.gov.au/Individuals/Super/Accessing-your-super/Early-access-to-your-super/

It is best to speak with an accountant or financial planner who has an Australian Financial Services License to discuss your options.

Investment Property in the Same Area

A Plan B if you are in a financial position is to buy an investment property in the same area you currently reside. This helps in the event you need to downsize or in the event of a relationship break up as you have either two homes, or an option to live without the immediate need to sell and repurchase.

Do you have the following documentation?	Yes or No	Action to take	By when?
Income Protection Insurance			
Mortgage Protection Insurance			
Title deed			
Loan documentation			
Building clearance certificates			
Market Valuation			

Key take-away:

All homes store memories, most of them pleasant and we all get a tinge of sadness when selling one. But the challenges intensify when it becomes imperative to sell a home under conditions which are anything but voluntary. The text and links above, together with the story below, are designed to help you plan for such an eventuality.

Story

Distressed Sale of a House – Melanie Macfarlane

Who knew life could take such a turn?

Back in 2006 I seemingly had it all. Life had been good since migrating to Australia in 2002, on the same plane departing London Heathrow airport as Kylie Minogue and my dog. 11 September 2002, one year after the big event in NYC, perhaps a sign that the next stage of my life was going to be a pretty important one. By September 2006 I had a great job building up an education consultancy business for the owner of a group of international education colleges in Sydney, a wonderful social life with lot of friends and fun, and was living in a lovely terrace house in Enmore with my partner of 10 years and our border collie, Bali, who had accompanied us on that plane journey from the UK 4 years prior. We had bought the house on the spur of the moment 18 months after migrating, with the proceeds of the apartment we sold in the UK prior to leaving. It was my doing, really. I fell in love with the frangipani tree out front and although Rob, my then partner, warned me of the immense work that needed to be done to it to make it truly habitable and comfortable, I did not listen, determined it was the right time for us to buy a house and that it would be a good investment. In some ways the house was our undoing. Rob is a builder by trade and therefore knew what he was talking about when he said there was a lot of work to be done. In the end we rented our house in Greenwich for about 3 more months whilst the work was going on in Enmore, bashing out walls and putting in beams to hold walls in place until finally we were ready to move in with no kitchen and a lot of takeaway dinners for a few weeks. There followed months of renovating, constantly being surrounded by, and caked in, dust, complaints from the neighbours and a lot of arguing between us. The reality of what we were doing was far from the idyll of the beautiful terrace with the frangipani tree that I had imagined. Rob was right, and that made it even worse.

The fact is, our relationship had always been a bit rocky, maybe more from my non-commital younger self. He was 9 years older than me and we had originally met in Sydney and got together on New Year´s Eve 1996, and moved back to Bournemouth UK, where he was from, shortly after this, when both our working holiday visas expired. He was the first guy I had lived with and it all happened so fast after we travelled back to the UK together via the Cook Islands, hitchhiking around New Zealand and an amazing over land trip through the US. We made a life for ourselves in Bournemouth and I liked a lot of his friends but never quite felt like it was the life I would have chosen for myself. I am not a natural follower I have realised, more of a leader. Three years later he asked to marry me on NYE in Edinburgh´s Princes St and my heart sank and I told him I wasn't ready. He was gutted and went off on a year-long motorbike trip around the world where I met up with him at various points for some amazing holidays, and a particularly memorable one in Darjeeling. Somehow, we kept going and then our permanent residence for Australia came through and we decided to go for it and travel together to the land of opportunity.

This time he was definitely following me. Looking back, I realise it was my decision and he would have been happy to stay put, despite his restless spirit. I yearned for a more adventurous and fulfilling life in Australia, having grown up in Vanuatu and always loved this part of the world, which has been like a second home, if not home itself. Not long after our arrival I got into singing and acting classes, dance and surf classes, started to make a whole bunch of great friends and started on my spiritual path with my organic dance class and the friends I made through this. I was in my element! Rob was not. He missed his mates, found it hard to get work initially, was generally dispirited and it just got worse. Buying the house together was once again a solution to keep our relationship going, since after all we had been together a number of years by now and it seemed the right step to take. A bit like having a child to patch up a relationship though; living through months of renovating; and my restlessness and need for distraction; and, frankly, healthy fun - seeing me dive out at any opportunity to my other life with all my spiritual dance mates and surf friends; this was not a recipe for success. Rob´s growing depression started to sour our relationship and his non-egalitarian side meant that our joint bank account kept diminishing as he would take a whole chunk of dollars out to buy himself a motorbike or two and I would find that instead of working on the house he had been out and about for days at a time with our neighbour who was a bit of a waster (and increasingly becoming a negative influence in Rob´s life). We started getting into credit card debt as Rob had less work outside of working on our house and my job was nowhere near enough to pay the mortgage.

By September 2006 I had had enough! I felt like my spirit was being crushed by the weight of all the pressure of the renovation, our financial situation; and Rob´s depression; and resentment towards me having any life outside of our relationship. A work trip to Latin America beckoned. I have to confess that I went wild on that trip, and I mean truly wild! Oh, those caipirinhas!! 'Highway to the Danger Zone' is a song title that springs to mind. After 4 weeks I returned a different person, South America unleashed something inside me and I told Rob I could not continue with our relationship. He would not accept this and was determined we would remedy our relationship. My parents were coming to stay from Scotland and he wanted us to put on a front. By this time, we were sleeping in separate bedrooms but given the house only had two bedrooms we would be forced to share a bedroom again. I was dreading this. Before my parents arrived, I phoned them and to my mother´s dismay I told them we were splitting up. My father, I discovered later, was relieved. He never believed Rob and I were suited, apparently! Very intuitive, my father. Obviously, deep down I had always known this too. There was something of the bully in Rob, for all his nice guy traits. In the meantime, I had booked a trip for a few days in December 2006, to take part in a fire festival in Hawaii along with some friends from my organic dance group.

I told Rob and my parents, when they arrived, that we would need to sell the house.

It was a hideous time. Rob was furious with me and I had deliberately made things worse by having a fling with a plumber from my organic dance class (I clearly had a thing for tradies back then – months later, after this initial 'rebound', I would have a six-month relationship with a mechanic) which he found out about. I was determined to saw our relationship in half. My parents were supportive, but it was very difficult for them to be in the middle of us. We had to pretend to the real estate agent that we were still together because we felt that they would just want to get rid of the house fast and it would influence the price we could get for it. I remember the real estate guy coming over one day and looking at the whiteboard I had put up in the kitchen sharing out our costs – I was so sick of losing all our money in our joint bank account, I had coerced Rob into setting up his own account and I had set my own account up and cancelled our joint one – he clearly must have suspected something was up. It made no difference anyway. My heart wasn't in it. The auction date could only be set for early December when I was going to be away in Hawaii. We had bought at a time when prices were peaking and sold at a bad time. Years later I think about how much that house is now worth and then stop myself thinking further!! Regardless, despite losing money in the sale, after all that we had put into renovating the house, I was just so relieved we were one step closer to being apart. What I didn´t know was that the worst was yet to come. Dividing the funds. I will never forget one lunch time after we had sold the house and moved our separate ways (in fact Rob had decided to return to England) and we met in a café to discuss the final proceeds. This was after I had agreed to a ridiculously unfair settlement where Rob accused me of having spent most of the money on our credit cards, not taking account of his motorbike purchases etc. Of course, the guilt I felt for having ended the relationship, the fling with the plumber, the wild time in Brazil, led me to agree to receiving less than one third of the amount we received from the sale of the house. In the end, in the café when Rob was threatening to go to a lawyer to get more money, I started crying, sobbing loudly with concerned onlookers sitting at tables around us, until Rob relented, and we agreed to our original division of the funds. To be honest the tears were genuine, but I suspect a part of me brought them on to appeal to Rob´s softer side. Knowing full well that bringing on board a lawyer would just see our funds dwindling to a ridiculously small amount, and I just wanted to cut my losses. Over the years I have felt angry at the way in which we settled things financially, particularly after I remembered that it had been my parents who gave us the deposit to put down on the apartment in England that we sold to have the funds to purchase a property in Australia, but I have long since gotten over this. I am just grateful I managed to find my freedom once more. 10 years in a relationship and this was what it came down to!

It did affect me though. I refused to ever have a joint bank account in the same way again. My husband and I have separate bank accounts and I use my own money to pay for my own needs. We pay for things jointly for our son and the house mortgage etc., but from our separate accounts. A client the other day told me that she and her partner had opened a joint bank account and would put all their salaries into it and use it as their only operating account, and I wanted to warn her of the implications!

The upshot of the story though is positive. As in previous stories in this book, it never rains but it pours. I carried on a disastrous rebound relationship with the plumber for a while, moved into a shared house with a friend who, I soon discovered, was a bit of an alcoholic, and my dog died a few months after this! My boss turned out to be a complete nightmare and by the middle of 2007 I had resigned. However – in South America I had met someone who offered me visa work and the chance to set up my own business, which I did after returning from a restorative trip to the UK, using the proceeds of the house sale to help finance my first three months until things really took off and frankly I have never looked back since. I met my husband a few months later and we now have a beautiful three-year-old son, a gorgeously cute labradoodle, and a thriving business together (he runs the education consultancy side, I the immigration side). We bought a house together two years ago using our pooled finances. This time it was fully renovated!! I did not plan to make that mistake again.

I hope that I have not painted my ex-partner to be an ogre. He certainly is not. We became friends again when I returned to the UK after our break up, and although we have completely lost touch now, he is with a partner and they have a son also and I am sure are living a happy life, much more suited to each other than the two of us were. I wish him all the best for the rest of his life. Both of us revealed our shadow sides to each other during our break up and distressed house sale.

Life has a funny way of turning out though, and I believe that there is always a positive side to everything!

Chapter 12

Documentation Checklist and Website Links

Plan B Documentation Checklist

Now you know what to be including in your Plan B you need to decide where you are going to keep all the documentation. There are several options available and whatever you decide by ensuring the documents can be accessed by those who you want when they need will ensure the choice is the correct one.

With the increased use of digital technology obtaining this information otherwise could be next to impossible. Think of all the passwords to the numerous websites you access on a daily basis, who else knows how to access this information?

Storage options

Now Sorted - www.nowsorted.com - is a highly secure, online storage facility, on Amazon servers, here in Australia. It's an ideal and safe repository for all your sensitive Plan B personal, family and business information. Now Sorted can easily – and safely – accommodate all the documents listed in the checklists that follow.

It strongly differentiates from other online storage sites in that, with one click, you can produce a handy (and, if you wish, shareable) *Crucial Facts Report & Directory* on all your key information and stored documents. The number of people and related entities you can store for is unlimited.

It also differentiates because you can invite up to five 'trusted others' to have limited (or unlimited – you decide) access to data and documents in case of emergencies. Everything is securely encrypted and available on any smart device (phone, tablet, etc) at any time. As Eddie Lees says, *'We designed this powerful app to help users prepare for any unexpected event – because there's always one around the corner'*. Eddie is the founder of Now Sorted Pty Ltd, and has strongly supported and encouraged the completion of this book.

Online Document Storage – consider using standard storage applications available online that have bank level security to store your records.

Paper records – keep original and copies in folder of the documents prepared. Ideally a safe, locked filing cabinet or in a secure location with the provision that someone knows how to access and locate this information.

Final Checklist

Documentation	Completed	Filed
Death	**Completed**	**Filed**
Will		
Life Insurance policy		
Birth Certificate		
Power of Attorney		
Enduring Power of Attorney		
Statement of Wishes		
List of assets		
List of liabilities		
Passwords		
Online access details		
Any information for the Funeral Service		
Death of a spouse or dependant	**Completed**	**Filed**
Will		
Life Insurance policy		
Birth certificate		
Power of Attorney		
Enduring Power of Attorney		
Statement of Wishes		
List of assets		
List of liabilities		
Password		
Online access details		
Any information for the Funeral Service		

Divorce – without kids	Completed	Filed
Agreed asset allocation and worst case scenario plan		
Prenuptial Agreement (if not signed under duress)		
Information on the joint family assets and income		
Contact details – lawyer, mediator,		
Information for useful organisations		
Marriage certificate		
Birth certificate		
Updated Superannuation Binding Nominations		
Financial position at date of marriage		

Divorce – with kids	Completed	Filed
Contact details – lawyer, mediator,		
Information and useful organisations		
Marriage certificate		
Birth certificate		
Birth certificates of children		
Children's passports		
Financial position at date of marriage		

Disability or incapacity due to accident or illness	Completed	Filed
Income Protection Insurance		
Total and Permanent Disability Cover		
Are you covered by workers' compensation insurance?		
Contact details – insurer, doctor, etc		

Dismissal from employment	Completed	Filed
Employment contract		
Timeline of events, performance review records and correspondence		
Contact details of lawyer, tribunal		
Do you have a financial safety net in the vent you are asked to leave work?		
Redundancy Insurance		
Access to other funds to cover everyday living expenses while you seek new employment?		

Disaster occurring whilst travelling	Completed	Filed
Travel Insurance		
Travel itinerary and contact details with a family member or friend		
Confirmation of details on Smartraveller		
Copy of passport		
Copy of birth certificate		
Copy of marriage or divorce certificates		
Copy of vaccination record		
First aid certificate		

Dissolution of a business for unforeseen or financial reasons	Completed	Filed
Business Plan		
Insurance		
Real time accounting records		
Risk management plan		
Original structure documentation ie trust deed, certificate of incorporation		
Business owner agreements		
Passwords for all business applications		

Back up of critical information		
Occupational Health and Safety records		
Any other required government or professional records ie tax agent registration, Certificate of Professional Practice etc		
Depression or mental illness	**Completed**	**Filed**
Income protection insurance		
Total and Permanent Disability Cover		
Trauma Insurance		
Power of Attorney		
Enduring Power of Attorney		
Advance care plan		
Password information for online applications with a close family member or friend		
Private Health Insurance		
Distressed Sale of Home	**Completed**	**Filed**
Income Protection Insurance		
Mortgage Protection Insurance		
Title deed		
Loan documentation		
Building clearance certificates		
Market Valuation		

Useful Website Information

Holmes and Rahe

1. Holmes and Rahe Stress online test - https://www.mindtools.com/pages/article/newTCS_82.htm

Death

1. Princelistofassets - http://www.mncourts.gov/mncourtsgov/media/CIOMediaLibrary/Documents/Inventory.pdf
2. Documents to prepare - https://www.moneysmart.gov.au/life-events-and-you/over-55s/wills-and-power-of-attorney
3. NSW Government Planning Ahead http://planningaheadtools.com.au/
4. NSW Government dying intestate - http://www.tag.nsw.gov.au/intestacy-faq-virtual.html
5. Online documentation storage - www.nowsorted.com
6. WA Government dying intestate https://www.legalaid.wa.gov.au/InformationAboutTheLaw/BirthLifeandDeath/Mattersafterdeath/Pages/Dyingwithoutawill.aspx
7. How to register organ donation - http://www.donatelife.gov.au/
8. Australian Government information on what to do following a death, this is a fantastic resource - https://www.humanservices.gov.au/customer/subjects/what-do-following-death

Death of a spouse or close family member

1. Australian Government information on what to do following a death, this is a fantastic resource - https://www.humanservices.gov.au/customer/subjects/what-do-following-death

Divorce – without kids

1. Divorce case - http://www.hcourt.gov.au/assets/cases/02-Brisbane/b14-2017/Thorne_SP.pdf
2. http://www.hcourt.gov.au/cases/case_b14-2017
3. Divorce app - https://thistoo.co/
4. Divorce app - https://amicable.io/

Divorce – with kids

1. Familycourtparentinginformation - http://www.familycourt.gov.au/wps/wcm/connect/fcoaweb/family-law-matters/family-law-in-australia/parenting-cases-the-best-interests-of-the-child
2. Applying to the court for orders fact sheet - http://www.familycourt.gov.au/wps/wcm/connect/fcoaweb/reports-and-publications/publications/court-orders/applying-to-the-court-for-orders
3. How do I – Apply for consent orders - http://www.familycourt.gov.au/wps/wcm/connect/fcoaweb/how-do-i/apps-orders/consent-orders/applying-consent-orders

Disability or incapacity due to accident or illness

4. Social media funding - https://au.gofundme.com/
5. Social media funding - https://mycause.com.au
6. Social media funding - https://gogetfundraising.com
7. SafeWork Australia - https://www.safeworkaustralia.gov.au/

Dismissal from employment

1. Australian Government department -www.fairwork.gov.au
2. Cases - https://www.fwc.gov.au/cases-decisions-and-orders.

Disaster occurring whilst travelling

1. Australian Government Department - http://dfat.gov.au/pages/default.aspx
2. Smartraveller - http://smartraveller.gov.au/

Dissolution of a business that is unforeseen or due to financial losses

1. Business Plan template https://www.business.gov.au/info/plan-and-start/templates-and-tools

Depression or mental illness – provided by Philipa Thornton

In an emergency call 000.

1. Lifeline 131114 - https://www.lifeline.org.au/
2. Your local mental health crisis team: https://www.healthdirect.gov.au/crisis-management
3. International help lines: http://www.iasp.info/resources/Crisis_Centres/
4. Beyond Blue https://www.beyondblue.org.au/
5. Black Dog Institute https://www.blackdoginstitute.org.au/
6. Buddhist Vipassana Retreat NSW and worldwide: http://www.internationalmeditationcentre.org/global/index.html
7. Richard Carlson's *Stop Thinking and Start Living*. https://www.goodreads.com/book/show/665846.Stop_Thinking_Start_Living_Discover_Lifelong_Happiness
8. Emmerson, G. (2012) *Healthy Parts Happy Self, 3 Steps to Like Yourself.* http://www.resourcetherapyinternational.com/store/p2/Healthy_Parts_Happy_Self_-_By_Gordon_Emmerson_PhD_%282012%29.html available here at a 20% discount follow instructions to download.

9. Headspace https://www.headspace.org.au
10. Healthy Place. https://www.healthyplace.com/
11. Neuman, G. (1999) *Helping your kids cope with divorce the Sandcastles way.* Random House: New York
12. http://mgaryneuman.com/books/helping-kids-cope-with-divorce-the-sandcastles-way/
13. Marriage Works http://marriageworks.com.au/
14. The Resource Therapy Institute of Australia (for mental health clinicians http://resourcetherapy.com.au/
15. Psych Solutions NSW www.psychsolutions.net.au
16. Rachel Naomi Remen http://www.rachelremen.com/books/kitchen-table-wisdom/
17. Rachel Naomi Remen's books https://onbeing.org/programs/rachel-naomi-remen-listening-generously/
18. *Sane* https://www.sane.org/mental-health-and-illness/facts-and-guides
19. Michael Sealey's Depression Relief Hypnosis & Meditation for 10 Days http://www.youtube.com/playlist?list=PLO9OtUmChpP9B0ENtvcz3YErx1rLs3kxN
20. Get therapy http://www.resourcetherapyinternational.com/find-a-resource-therapist-in-australia--worldwide.html
21. EMDR http://www.emdr.com/what-is-emdr/
22. Radical Exposure tapping http://www.radicalexposure.com/
23. Andrew Solomon - https://youtu.be/-eBUcBfkVCo
24. Psychologist Susan Heitler - https://youtu.be/_re6AX3Mi4s
25. Yoga laughter http://laughteryoga-australia.org/

Distressed sale of home

1. Early access to superannuation - https://www.ato.gov.au/Individuals/Super/Accessing-your-super/Early-access-to-your-super/

Contributors to 'Planning Plan B'

Accountant

Lotus Accountants – Kylie Parker

Kylie has had an extremely rewarding career as a Chartered Accountant assisting clients accumulate personal wealth through her knowledge of tax law and business. However, accumulation is not enough – you need to know how to protect both your wealth and your family in times of crisis. That belief has led to writing Planning Plan B.

Counsellor

Marriage Works - Phillipa Thornton

Philipa is an extremely well qualified relationship psychologist, Clinical Supervisor of psychologists and the director of Marriage Works, a busy therapy practice designed to help couples and individuals gain relief from the heartache of relationship distress. Philipa believes you deserve to heal from emotional pain and have healthy loving relationships in your life. Philipa is Vice President of Resource Therapy International and her views on relevant issues are much sought after.

Document management, organisation and secure online storage

Now Sorted Pty Ltd – Eddie Lees

Following a successful career in financial services, Eddie's team developed a solution for the challenge every family faces: *"If you get hit by a bus, how will I know how and where all our personal and business information and documents fit together. Seriously, how will I know?"* Now Sorted is the remarkable result. (**www.nowsorted.com**)

Financial planner

Priority Advisory Group – Mark Bradley and Hamish Thomson

Mark and Hamish work with a team of passionate advice professionals who seek to make a positive difference in other people's lives. Priority Advisory Group help individuals, families and SMEs identify their needs and objectives then develop and implement strategies designed to achieve their objectives. Priority Advisory Group seek to build long term partnerships with clients and "partner with them for a better life

Foundation

Nicole Fitzsimons Foundation – Kate Fizsimons

Kate is one of AFR/Westpac's 100 Women of Influence, a Motivational Speaker, Certified Life Coach and Director of the Nicole Fitzsimons Foundation - established in honour of her sister who was killed in an overseas accident. She passionately shares her story at high schools to educate students about the importance of travel safety and building resilience to overcome adversity. Being described as 'eye-opening' and 'life-changing', her presentations have reached over 50,000 students and counting.

Insurance companies

Bizcover – Michael Gottlieb

Michael is an experienced 'start up' entrepreneur who has founded 4 insurance businesses since 2001, all of which have repeatedly won accolades in the insurance & technology arenas. Michael's key focus is on BizCover, which is Australia & NZ's only commercial insurance service where SME clients can instantly compare & buy their insurance online from leading insurers. To date they have helped over 150,000 clients. Out of work, Michael and his wife Kerry have 3 beautiful children.

Experien – Mark Sacks

Mark, is an award-winning life insurances and income protection specialist broker since 2004 who has helped many people and families who have encountered unexpected events such as illness, disability and premature death with their insurance claims for policies they had implemented. Through this he has witnessed how powerful insurance has been to claimants.

Understand Insurance – Campbell Fuller

Understand Insurance is an initiative of the Insurance Council of Australia, the peak body for the general insurance industry. Understand Insurance gives consumers and small businesses practical information to help them understand general insurance and make informed decisions.

Law firms

Barkus Doolan – Melinda Winning

Melinda has experience in a wide variety of family law matters including property, spouse maintenance, child support, international child abduction and complex parenting cases. Melinda's wealth of experience allows her to approach all aspects of her practice with a view to achieving the best possible outcome for clients either through mediation or litigation.

Nexus Lawyers - Alan Prasad

Alan is a corporate and commercial services lawyer with extensive experience and specialisation in mergers, acquisitions, corporate/business structures, employment, intellectual property, regulatory and compliance, franchising and, commercial dispute resolutions.

In Memory OF

Chris – Brother in law, died at 31 leaving behind a wife and 2 children aged 7 & 5 when a young driver fell asleep at the wheel veering into the path of Chris on his motorbike, he was killed instantly.

Jean – Paternal Grandmother – died at 84, dementia and aged care nursing

Pauline – Mother in law, died at 59 of breast cancer

Emily – Friend, died at 24 in a car accident in NZ with her boyfriend

Tom – Friend, died at 24 travelling, fell off a train late at night with an unlocked carriage door

Sid – Maternal Grandfather, died at 84 suffering Parkinson's and in a nursing home

Bill – my Dad, died at 59 of cancer after an 18-month decline

Lorna – my Nan, died at 87, went into coma in her sleep with her beloved Chihuahua Leo beside her. Our family all got to say goodbye.

Nicole – Friends daughter, died at 24, travelling in Thailand on the back of a scooter when it was hit by a speeding driver

Murray – Friend, died at 53 of cancer

To my ex Husbands

No. 1 - I am sorry, we went through too much too young

No. 2 – I know you're sorry, you at least gave me two beautiful boys and continue to be a good Dad

To my ex Business Partners

I believe in Karma, I just wish it would Karma Fasta

Acknowledgements

To all my friends, family, clients and professional colleagues without whom my life would not be as rich, fun or funny. Experiencing the hard times in life does sort the wheat from the chaff and I am so blessed to have such deep personal connections through all areas of my life.

Adam, having first met when we were at the peak of our confidence and youth to re connect in our 40's and find a relationship that we didn't know could be possible, is an example of when there is no planning for Plan A or Plan B. Sometimes life just happens unexpectedly and not in a bad way, not in a perfect way, but different, better, with new challenges and new rewards.

To the people who helped me through my "annus horribilis" by keeping me sane. Some of you are contributors in this book, some were fleeting relationships found online but it is amazing how supported I have felt through my own massive changes in my personal and business life. I'd like to thank Charissa Gannon, Bridget Francis and Claire Palmer for providing support above and beyond friendship, Robert Rochlin, Julie Muldowney, Caitlyn Barnier and Lara Scott for holding me together professionally, Rob Stone for giving me the opportunity at Xero, Don Peers for being a fantastic Yoga teacher and patient listener, my business networking friends that have turned into wining and dining friends and to everyone who has had to listen to me vent. I can never thank you enough for without you I have no doubt I would have fallen into a very dark depression at the start of 2015.

Contributors

My heartfelt thanks to all the experts and people who have shared their very personal stories and their professional expertise in the aim of helping others prepare for life's unexpected stressful events.

Alan Prasad	Campbell Fuller
Hamish Thomson	Kate Fitzsimons
Mark Sacks	Mark Bradley
Melanie McFarlane	Melinda Winning
Michael Gottlieb	Michael Long
Philipa Thornton	Vanessa Billy

Reviewers and Constructive Feedback

Thanks for being brave and kind with your suggestions and improvements.

Adam Harris	Eddie Lees
Sholto Macpherson	Simone Macks

www.ingramcontent.com/pod-product-compliance
Lightning Source LLC
Chambersburg PA
CBHW051944290426
44110CB00015B/2105